The Man Who Killed Houdini

The Man Who Killed
HOUDINI

Don Bell

Véhicule Press

Published with the generous assistance of The Canada Council for the Arts, the Book Publishing Industry Development Program of the Department of Canadian Heritage, and the Société de développement des entreprises culturelles du Québec (SODEC).

There were many people and institutions who generously provided Don Bell with information and images for this book. Unfortunately, some of these records were lost when the author passed away in 2003. The publisher will be pleased to acknowledge any contribution in future editions of the book.

Cover design: J.W. Stewart
Set in Adobe Minion by Simon Garamond
Printed by Marquis Book Printing Inc.
Front cover photo of Houdini is a detail from Souvenir Program, Coast-to-coast tour 1926-27.
Photo of Houdini opp. title page courtesy of Magic Tom Auburn
Photo of author by Elke Abrell

LIBRARY AND ARCHIVES CANADA CATALOGUING IN PUBLICATION

Bell, Don, 1936-2003.
    The man who killed Houdini / Don Bell.

ISBN 1-55065-187-0

I. Houdini, Harry, 1874-1926—Death. II. Whitehead, J. Gordon.
I. Title.

GV1545.H8B44 2004   793.8'092   C2004-904017-0

Véhicule Press
www.vehiculepress.com

US DISTRIBUTION
Independent Publishers Group
814 North Franklin Street, Chicago, IL 60610
800.888.4741 / orders@ipgbook.com / www.ipgbook.com

CANADIAN DISTRIBUTION
LitDistCo Distribution, 100 Armstrong Avenue,
Georgetown, Ontario L7G 5S4 / 800.591.6250 / orders@litdistco.ca

Printed and bound in Canada

For Valérie and Oliver; Daniel, Bing, and Julien;
and Odile and Ugo

One day my father [novelist Morley Callaghan] asked me, "Who killed all the magic, who killed Harry Houdini?" He had to tell me. He said a Canadian killed Harry Houdini – just stepped out of nowhere in a crowd and punched him in the stomach and killed him.
    –Barry Callaghan in *Books in Canada*, 1993

As I understand it, he was caught off guard.
    –Richard Déry, Customs inspector

Criminal charges were never filed against Whitehead, and what became of him isn't known.
    –William Barrett, Montreal *Gazette*, October 31, 1986

"Murdered."
"Murdered?"
"Yes, murdered."
    –Movie quip in *Saturday Evening Post*

Contents

Acknowledgments

Many people helped in the research and writing of this book. I would like to sincerely and enthusiastically thank the following persons and apologize to those whose names are missing due to lapsed memory or lost notes. The list is in alphabetical order. My thanks to:

Tevia Abrams, Sandy Amos, Katherine Anslow, Wally Aspell, Magic Tom Auburn, Hilda Baker, Mary Bancroft, Dr. William Barakett, Maurice Barker, Dr. Philip Belitsky, Roslyn Belitsky, Daniel Bell, Valérie Bell, Norman Bigelow, Harry Blank, Richard Bolton, Dr. Munro Bourne, Ruth Brandon, Dan Bruce, Mario Carrardi Jr., Catherine Clarke, Kevin Clarke, Gerald Cohen, Maureen Cohen, Dr. William Cohen, John Robert Colombo, Robert Coull, Carolyn DaPonti, Dr. Michel Dansereau, Richard Déry, Kathy Dezene, John Doig, Bruce Dolphon, Leon Edel, Barbara Layton Elvidge, Ted Ferguson, Eva Fieldman, Ron Finegold, Ann Fisher, F.G. Flynn, Maureen Forrester, Turner Fumerton, Dr. Pierre Gagné, Dr. Wilfred Gallay, Doris Gauthier, Walter Gibson, Clyde Gilmour, Percy Goldberg, Trudis Goldsmith, Versa Greene (Mabel Jackson), Rev. Canon J.A. Greenhalgh, Donald Gresko, Nora Hague, Archie Handel, Stanley Handman, Marcus Handman, Jo-Ann Harding, Jack Hausner, Tilya Helfield, Nguyen Van Hiep, Joan Higbee, Doris Hoe, Pam Holgate, Michael Horn, Del Hushell, Andrew Jaquays, Charles Jaquays, Mort Jaquays, Mort Jaquays Jr., John Jennings, Norma Jennings, Mike Jurkowski, Edith Knowles, Joyce La Judice, Dick Langstrath, Gilles Larin, Marcel Larin, Phil Layton, Peggy Leatherbarrow, Ceil Lewonchuk, Angus McLeod, Graham McKeen, Alf McKergow, Duncan McWhirter, Karen Virginia Mann, David Marler, Alice Martin, Dr. George Maughan, Thomas "Bert" McConnell, Christine McKay, Robert Michel, Etta Miller, Ivie Miller, Ian Moggs, Brian Moores, Gerald Morgan, Henry Muller, Harry Napier, Gordon Nelles, Lloyd Newman, Adelaide Edythe North, Favery O'Connor, Odile Perret, Dr. Eric Phelps, Marian Phelps, Annette Pickleman, Avrom Podbere, Janice Grossman Pollack, Nettie Posen, Saul Posen, Eldred Post,

John D. Powell, Jacques Price, Syd Radner, Laurie (Jackson) Reid, Robert Richard, Rod Riordan, Gerald Robitaille, Frances Rodick, Jack Rodick, Lola Ross, Karen Rowantree, Daniel Ryan, Dr. Joseph Scales, Theresa Scales, Ethel Schatz, Tommy Schnurmacher, Rev. Bernice Seaborn, Audrey Searcy, Barry Shiller, Charles Smiley, Sam Smiley, Doris Soobis, Benjamin Spellman, Mike Spinnard, Dr. Werner Spitz, Norman Tibbetts, Tom Tietse, Jim Tolve, David Turkington, Doreen Turner, Marie Vanasse, Leonard Warshaw, Manny Weltman, J. Ralph Whitehead, Reg Whitehead, Stanley Whitehead, Harry Wong Jr., Helen Wong, Katie Wong, Raymond Wong, John Xinos, Dorothy Young, Earl Zuckerman.

INTRODUCTION

Man of Magic

~

MY HUNT for Harry Houdini's assassin began in 1982. It is well known that he died in Detroit, at age fifty-two, on Halloween day in 1926, nine days after being sucker-punched in the stomach. Various accounts claim the assailant was an amateur boxer, a football player, a Montreal newspaperman, a *McGill Daily* reporter, a medical student, a divinity student.

It is said, although it's hard to find corroboration of this, that Houdini used to boast that he could withstand any blow to his abdomen by tensing his muscles beforehand, by putting mind over matter. According to the story rendered in most biographies (for instance, the classic *Houdini: The Untold Story* by Milbourne Christopher), the magician was caught off-guard, like a boxer being swatted while still on his stool.

Was he unprepared this one time?

Was it an accident, or foul play?

This book is not a biography of the amazing illusionist and escape artist whose name is entrenched in our language: to pull a "Houdini" has come to mean "to escape from a seemingly inextricable predicament", especially by using one's wits. *Funk and Wagnall's Standard English Dictionary* even acknowledges a verb form. "To houdinize" is "to release … oneself from [confinement, bonds, or the like], as by wiggling out." Regularly his name appears in descriptive passages in newspapers. A miraculous sea rescue is described as "a Houdini-like act". A globe-trotting diplomat is called "the Houdini of American foreign policy". Screams a tabloid headline: "Magician Saws Girl In Half—Amateur Houdini Bungles Trick As Audience Watches in Horror."

There's no dearth of books on Houdini, and any inquisitive reader interested in finding out about his spectacular escapes from manacles, straitjackets, airtight containers lowered into treacherous seas, and every conceivable constricting device, or his causing elephants to disappear from a Broadway stage with one whoosh of his magic wand, need only check out second-hand bookstores and libraries. Our purpose here is to inquire into the mystery of the magician's death.

The craving to find out about the puncher and the witnesses became a full-blown obsession. It developed after a more or less routine assignment for *Today* Magazine, a Canadian weekly newspaper supplement, which ran a regular feature in the early 1980s called "I Was There," where witnesses to major historic or catastrophic events would give a first-person narrative of what they saw and experienced. One of the editors, John Doig, thought it would make an enchanting "I Was There" feature if somebody who was with Houdini in Montreal or who witnessed the famous punching episode could be found. *Today*'s collapse unfortunately took place shortly after the story had been assigned.

But the die was cast. I had already begun plunging into biographies, essays, and newspaper features about Houdini's Montreal-connected death.

Houdini was vigorously exposing the fraudulent methods of spiritualists in his lectures and writings and on the stage. Was it just a coincidence that his demise occurred at a moment when spiritualists were prophesying his doom, some even threatening him with physical harm if he didn't let up? One Houdini foul-play theorist has gone so far as to describe his death as "a spiritualist contract killing."

My inquiry went in bursts from 1982 onward. Especially around Halloween each year it seemed as if Houdini were calling me, from wherever he was, to sniff around for new clues. Then roundabout every fourth year for some reason there seemed to be an orgy of intense research: in 1982 when it began and Sam Smiley, who was in the dressing room, told his story; 1986 when the first serious attempts were made to find the other witness, Jacques Price, and the assailant, J. Gordon Whitehead; 1990 when much more was found out about both of them and about other events that took place when Houdini played Montreal; then through the first half of the 1990s as a host of new characters entered the frame and new theories came to light.

The trail heated up. When I was least expecting it, the phone would ring, a letter would appear from some old-timer or the offspring of so-and-so who had heard about the investigation and wanted to add a twist, an untold tale. Somebody who knew the mysterious J. Gordon White-head, or of someone else who "tested" Houdini. These new leads arose magically, like Houdini himself arising from one of his chambers, out of the airtight past.

And now through the magic of the printed word we transport you to the Princess Theatre in Montreal. It is October 1926. Houdini is about to perform …

LADIES-AND-GENTLEMEN-LET'S-HAVE-A-GREAT-BIG-HAND-NOW-INTRODUCING-THE-ONE-AND-ONLY-THE HANDCUFF-KING-HERE-HE-IS-BACK-FROM-THE-GRAVE-THE-AMAZING-THE-MYSTIFYING-MR.-HARRY-HOUDINI!

1

Somebody Was Out to Get Him

$\sim$

WHEN HARRY HOUDINI performed at Montreal's Imperial Theatre in April 1925, and at the Princess in October 1926, Montreal was a wide-open night city, one of the top vaudeville entertainment centres in North America. As Jockey Fleming, the famous moocher who usually begged at the corner of Peel and Ste. Catherine, but probably worked the doors of the Princess when Houdini was in town, once remarked, "Everybody who is everybody came through like stinkbombs."

The "stinkbomb" list included Al Jolson, Eddie Cantor, Sacha Guitry—all the biggest names in 1920s showbiz. They usually brought their touring companies up to Montreal as soon as they closed in New York, four hundred miles straight north through the Adirondacks and then across the mighty St. Lawrence. A city in another country where marquees blazed all year round and entertainment-hungry show-goers thronged to the downtown palaces even during winter's worst ice epidemics and snowathons. Vibrant and burbling, Montreal had certainly changed since Mark Twain passed through in 1881 and observed, "This is the first time I was ever in a city where you can't throw a brick without breaking a church window."

With its three-humped mountain protruding from its core like magic mounds, Montreal was rich in culture, joie de vivre, and Old-World atmosphere, as foreign and exotic as you could get without crossing an ocean. For entertainers like Houdini who were interested in mind and body adventures as much as the glories of show business, it was a paradise. The hotels were first rate, the cuisine superb. The city's charm was epitomized by its flamboyant Mayor Médéric Martin, "Le grand Médéric," a cigar-maker with a working-class background who rose to top office and joyfully rode in state through downtown streets with the likes of the Prince of Wales and the Queen of Rumania.

Besides the theatres with their line-ups of top-drawer entertainment—not just vaudeville but also "pictures" (talkies were just coming into their own), plays, and opera—the city had museums and art and antique galleries catering to every taste. Of interest to Houdini, one of North America's top universities, McGill, was smack in the centre. The faculty of McGill includes personages like the renowned humourist Stephen Leacock, the eminent physician Sir William Osler, and the physicist Lord Ernest Rutherford who revolutionized scientific understanding of the atom. It also gave the world the nineteenth-century mutilator, poisoner of prostitutes, and prime Jack the Ripper candidate Dr. Thomas Neill Cream (no less a savant than Leacock earnestly believed Cream was the Ripper).

Today the Princess Theatre is the semi-chic art-deco style Le Parisien, a six-cinema complex showing first-run French-language films and the main venue of the Montreal World Film Festival. In Houdini's day it was an ornate, cavernous 2,200-seat auditorium—"the amusement centre of Montreal," as it described itself in coming-attractions ads. Inside, enormous murals depicted the spirit of music and enchantment, and sumptuous Italian-style draperies looped around the stage, the box seats, and the twin balconies. It was the ultimate in theatrical opulence. Besides offering "high-class vaudeville twice daily," it featured such popular silent movies as *The Four Horsemen of the Apocalypse*—the film that made Rudolph Valentino a star premiered at the Princess, as did *Michel Stroghoff*, the screen version of Jules Vernes' Cossack epic, one of the first movies produced "in natural colours."

It was located on Ste. Catherine Street a block east of Phillips Square and more or less across the street from Henry Morgan's Department Store where one Joscelyn Gordon Whitehead, a tall chisel-faced man in his thirties wearing a mackintosh, would be stopped by a house detective in 1928 for shoplifting books—a curious incident, perverse in some ways, about which more will be said.

Houdini was engaged to perform eight shows at the Princess, starting

Monday, October 18 and continuing through Saturday, October 23, with matinees Wednesday and Saturday. It was billed as "The Most Novel Entertainment Ever Staged—2 ½ Hours of Magic, Illusion, Escapes and Fraudulent Medium Exposés … It will sweep you off your feet and transport you to a land you never knew existed … See the Celebrated Chinese Water Torture Cell, the East Indian Needle Trick, Numerous Baffling Thrilling Mysteries."

Houdini's charm and outspokenness must have appealed to vaudeville-goers almost as much as his illusions. In 1926, his name was constantly in the news because of his impassioned campaign to expose the tricks being used by fraudulent spirit mediums to gull the public. In fact, the entire third act of his show was devoted to a demonstration of their manipulations. Every indication was that the show would be a smashing success. Montrealers loved big stars, and Houdini, at the peak of his career, was the biggest and best.

The "novel entertainment" he now had on tour was the dream of his life. Little did he know that other than one performance a week later in Detroit, where he collapsed on the stage of the Garrick Theatre, the performances at the Princess would be his last.

Somebody may have been out to get him. Being a magician, Houdini knew how spirit mediums, so popular in the nineteenth and early twentieth centuries, could use trickery to exploit supplicants who sought them out to make contact with departed loved ones. Clients could be persuaded to fork over fistfuls of money, thankful for the messages that they believed was genuine psychic voice-mail.

It is well known that Houdini's crusade began some time after his mother's death in 1913. There was nothing he would have liked more than for his beloved Cecilia to send him a sweet word or two from the beyond. He attended various séances, opening himself, as he later insisted, at least to the possibility that he would receive a message from Cecilia, but nothing came through that, as a rational man, he could feel convinced was his mother legitimately trying to reach him from another realm. Sir Arthur Conan Doyle's engagingly psychic wife, Lady Doyle, staged a séance for Houdini's benefit to try to bring back Mom. With the shades drawn the three of them sat around a séance table, Lady Doyle furiously scribbling messages which she claimed to be receiving from Houdini's mother on the psychic hotline. Not even then did Houdini bite. He couldn't imagine that his Cecilia, who in life on this earth spoke a broken Yiddish-accented English, would be sending out messages (conveyed through Lady Doyle's automatic writing) in sentence-perfect King's English, or that she would fail to mention it was her birthday on the day of the séance, or that, being an Orthodox Jew, she would have responded at all when Lady Doyle started recording her murmurings only after making the sign of the cross.

"I was willing to believe, even wanted to believe," Houdini said in his book *A Magician among the Spirits*. But he realized that his mother's death left a void that could not be filled by turning out the lights and placing his hands on a séance table, and that as much as he respected his renowned friend Conan Doyle, who invented a clever forensic detective named Sherlock Holmes, and his weird psychic wife, he too was being duped like all the other distressed mourners who left their credulity outside the medium's door.

Always quick to take up a cause, and a self-promoter throughout his career, Houdini started his relentless campaign to expose sham "communicators." He showed how they used props, illusions, manipulations, and accomplices to create mesmerizing effects in darkened séance rooms. Disembodied voices, bells chiming, tambourines clonking, messages scrawled on slate boards, blobs of so-called ectoplasm oozing off walls, tables levitating—of course Houdini knew all the "tricks" of the trade and often where they got their gadgets. He had a longstanding offer of $10,000 that he would donate to charity if any medium produced phenomena which he could not duplicate "by natural means."

Many spirit mediums were being driven out of business by Houdini's disclosures and denunciations. Their message to the great mystifier—to them not a mystifier but a pain in the spiritbody—was clear. A spiriting away to that other world for you, Mr. Houdini, where there are no podiums and platforms for screeching about our so-called unscrupulous methods, which you may not believe in, but we do.

The notorious Margery of Boston, the "Witch of Beacon Hill," even predicted in December 1924 through her spirit guide Walter that Houdini would be dead in less than a year. If he lasted close to two years after this dire prophecy, perhaps it was due less to an error in her clairvoyance than to Houdini's great resiliency and tenacity. He was, for sure, an escape artist.

Houdini in letters and conversations declared that the fraudulent mediums had plans to do him in. He knew that they would go to any ends to stop him. In his book *Margery the Medium* he quotes the slinky and alluring Picton, Ontario-born medium, wife of the wealthy Boston surgeon Dr. LeRoi Goddard Crandon, her benefactor and accomplice, as warning him, "Houdini, if you misrepresent me from the stage of the Keith's [Theatre in Boston], some of my friends will come and give you a good beating." Houdini, as it turned out, was given a good beating. Was Margery's just a playful threat? "When I die," Houdini was often quoted as saying, "the fraudulent mediums will declare the day a national holiday."

Houdini's string of bad luck began in Providence, Rhode Island the first week of October 1926. The lady he loved second only to his mother, his wife Beatrice—Bess—his "good luck charm" as he called her, fell ill with ptomaine poisoning.

After one of his shows, Houdini and Bess had dinner with lifelong Providence resident H.P. Lovecraft. The writer of disquieting horror tales was ghost-writing a column for Houdini in *Weird Tales* called "Ask Houdini." He also wrote articles on astrology and witchcraft and a book called *The Cancer of Superstition*, "which," Houdini announced, "would slay the dragon of occult fakery once and for all." One wonders what was on the menu that evening. Vegetables with ghastly creatures inside them as Lovecraft might have described in one of his lurid tales? Or had Bess, who by all accounts had a fondness for alcohol, gone overboard on the champagne that the boys offered her? The poet in me likes to imagine that it was after this repast with Lovecraft, "the master of terror, fantastic strangeness, and horror beyond the mind's range," as the backflap of *Dragon and Other Macabre Tales* describes him, that Houdini's calamities began.

Bess came down with an extremely high fever; Houdini, frantic, made a hurried phone call to New York to summon Sophie Rosenblatt, a nurse who had attended Mrs. Houdini in the past. Bess's temperature kept rising; Houdini sat with her throughout Friday night. On Saturday, the last day of his engagement at Providence's Opera House, her fever thankfully abated. Houdini supervised the packing of his paraphernalia for Albany, the next stop on the tour, and arranged for Bess to go directly to Albany with her nurse. He would keep appointments he had that weekend in New York, most notably with his lawyer, Bernard Ernst, to discuss libel actions amounting to more than $200,000 instigated against him by various irate spiritualists.

It was a gruelling few days. After a long overnight train journey from Providence to New York, he got little sleep in Manhattan except for a snooze on Ernst's living-room sofa while waiting for the lawyer. He was doubly burdened with all the details that Bess usually attended to. There were pieces of magic apparatus to buy or refurbish, more business meetings, and frequent worried phone calls to Albany to inquire about Bess.

It is believed that Houdini was in excellent health at the beginning of this tour. Sir Arthur Conan Doyle wrote that so far as bodily health goes, Houdini was as fit as any man of fifty-two could possibly be: "He was in constant training and used neither alcohol nor tobacco." Still, by the time he reached Albany after another slow overnight train, even with his superhuman strength and stamina, he was exhausted; he had hardly slept for three days and nights.

On opening night in Albany, during preparations for the difficult Chinese Water Torture Cell trick, came the second mishap. In the stunt Houdini was lowered head-first, his feet clamped in mahogany stocks, into a glass-fronted cage filled with water, and he was padlocked in. A curtain was drawn over the Torture Cell. When nobody could believe he was still alive, the curtain was pulled away to reveal Houdini standing outside the tank, water streaming from his body, the manacles inside the tank, still locked.

He'd performed the trick countless times without any glitches, but this time, as his assistants pulled on the ropes to hoist him feet-first into the cell, the frame suddenly jerked and he felt a spasm of pain shooting through his left ankle. Writhing, Houdini signalled his assistant to lower him. When he had completed the trick, his face was twisted in pain. Many people in the audience thought it was part of the drama. He asked if there was a doctor in the house. There was a bone specialist, as it happened, who examined him in the wings and told him his ankle most likely was fractured, although it would be hard to say how badly except with x-ray pictures. "You will have to go to the hospital at once," the doctor told him.

"Nothing doing," said Houdini. He waved his hand toward the over-flowing auditorium. "They paid their money, and I'll see the show through." He hobbled back to the footlights—only his right foot would support him—and asked the audience to allow him enough time to change out of his bathing suit into his evening clothes for the third act. He was given an enormous ovation; now everyone knew something had really gone wrong. Luckily there was a minimum of exertion in his medium-bashing last act, and it was his right foot that did all the manoeuvring of the props under the "séance table" as he demonstrated how the spirit-fakers performed.

It was confirmed at Albany's Memorial Hospital that Houdini's ankle was broken. It was reset and doctors advised him to stay off his feet for at least a week. Never one to heed medical advice, and believing of course in mind over matter—and being Houdini—he sat up all night in his hotel room fashioning a brace to support his injured leg. He filled his three-day engagement in Albany and moved on to Schenectady for the rest of the week.

The Schenectady *Gazette* promoted Houdini's show with an ad for "The Greatest Necromancer of the Age, Perhaps All Time." The word "necromancer" suggests black magic, sorcery, and communication with the dead. Houdini? The ad shows a drawing of bats, a witch, a black cat, and a gravestone. One wonders if this too was part of the writing-on-the-wall atmosphere, foreshadowing the events at his next port of call, Montreal.

There were rumours after he died that Houdini had severe stomach pains on the train that left Schenectady for Montreal and that he vomited during the trip. This was denied in an affidavit filed by his private secretary, Julia Sauer, who said she saw Houdini every day during his tour and swore that he was "in robust health … and so far as I know, not ill or suffering from any indisposition." Other members of the entourage also stated that, other than the injury to his ankle, he was in excellent physical condition. Nevertheless, whether Houdini had already been stricken with some serious abdominal problems before he received the blows in Montreal has long been a subject of debate amongst Houdini scholars.

In Montreal Houdini mystified his audience that opening Monday with his repertoire of magic feats and escape stunts during the first two acts. He seemed perfectly adroit even with his injured foot. The controversial third act was entirely devoted to demonstrating tricks employed by unscrupulous mediums. He went after them hammer and tongs, impressing the mostly worshipful members of the audience.

The Montreal *Daily Star*'s eminent theatre critic, S. Morgan Powell, wrote a glowing review that appeared in Tuesday's paper.

The extent to which the mysteries of magic and the field of the occult fascinate humanity was notably exemplified at the Princess Theatre last night, when an audience that packed every corner of the edifice, overflowed into the promenade at the rear, occupied extra chairs, and stood for three hours, watched with the closest and undivided attention the feats of that master-magician, Houdini, as he gave them a display of legerdemain, illusions, mysteries and the most astounding of tricks, concluding with an exposé of the fraudulent spiritist mediums who batten upon a gullible public—for cash.

… Houdini's hand has lost no whit of its former cunning … his entertainment never palls, no matter what he may be doing— whether he is drawing interminable yards of multi-coloured silk out of a goldfish bowl, or whisking alarm clocks across the stage from one hook to another by a wave of his arms, or producing rabbits, pigeons and fowls from some fourth dimension of space his audience cannot see.

Much of Powell's write-up focused on the third act:
[He] is absolutely serious when he discusses these alleged spiritists

relying upon the well-known credulity of the masses, who, he declares, are driving men and women to the madhouse, who are deceiving the poor, and who are taking advantage of every form of human frailty in belief to fill their pockets.

During his show Houdini went after not only well-known mediums like Margery of Boston, but also local charlatans. He described to his audience how he sent out his agents weeks ahead to investigate the mediums. One of them even used the name "F. Raud" and the mediums never batted an eyelid. Houdini interrogated his agents, who were sitting in the box seats during the show, about their visits to the Montreal mediums. "The agents were so completely convincing," wrote S. Morgan Powell, "as to make people marvel how anybody with a grain of common sense could possibly swallow such rubbish for a second."

Houdini called out names of various members of the audience, many of them involved in the social and commercial life of Montreal, and to their amazement recounted details of their lives as if he had an all-knowing sixth sense. Of course it was his spies, he cheerfully revealed, who had passed the information they had gleaned in their snooping on to him. The same means, he said, were within reach of any quack who desired to fleece an innocent public of its money.

"The mediums," S. Morgan Powell concluded, "will be hiding carefully until Houdini has gone. Deception cannot stand the light of truth that he brings to bear."

This vehement ridicule, one can guess, did not sit well with Montreal spiritualists. Like their counterparts in the United States, they no doubt would heave a collective sigh of relief and be dancing on broomsticks in the streets if Houdini had an "accident"; if he somehow left them in peace to go about their business.

During the early days of this inquiry, I heard about an elderly medium in Montreal who boasted that she had predicted Houdini's death, as did some of her colleagues. Was Houdini walking into a trap? Were there dark forces at work behind the scenes, already planning the national day of celebration?

On October 21, 1926 a Montrealer named James P. Clarke sent a letter to Conan Doyle in London after seeing Houdini's show. Though Doyle and Houdini had been friends, each admiring the other's talents, they'd had a falling out after Houdini had publicly, more than once, mocked Sir Arthur's fanatical endorsement of spirit entities. Doyle even suggested, much to Houdini's amusement, that the magician himself had supernatural gifts which enabled him to dematerialize at will and escape from any constricting apparatus.

The letter was published in 1933 in the book *Houdini and Conan Doyle: The Story of a Strange Friendship*, co-written by Houdini's lawyer Bernard Ernst and Hereward Carrington. Clarke told how Houdini had insulted Doyle during the show, calling him "just a 'writer of detective stories' who was eaten up by one subject. Furthermore, he said Doyle acted like a 'big school boy' at a conference [on spiritualism] in New York." The letter grows increasingly hostile toward Houdini when Clarke reports to Doyle that Houdini also said that Doyle would believe anything. Clarke thought Houdini's remarks were contemptuous and exceedingly unfair.

> And now I come to the most important part. As a final retort he said he wished you were there in front of him. He would "tear you to ribbons." Obviously he was taking advantage of the distance between London and Montreal. As these remarks were passed publicly, before a large crowd, I think it only right you should know of them. I was crowded down when I indignantly objected—he had the crowd with him. I felt I could not let this go without remark, since it might hurt your reputation here in Montreal. I could not tolerate the unfair and insolent manner in which he described you.

Who was James P. Clarke? No one with that exact name is listed in the 1926 *Lovell's City Directory*. Joscelyn Gordon Whitehead, it was later discovered, wrote letters to prominent persons. Could it have been Whitehead himself stalking Houdini, hiding under a pseudonym?

On page one of the *McGill Daily* student newspaper for Tuesday, October 19, the day after Houdini opened in Montreal, is a story based on an interview with Houdini in his Princesss Theatre dressing room by an enterprising reporter, twenty-two-year-old Gordon Nelles. That day, Houdini was scheduled to lecture about fraudulent mediums to students at the McGill Union Ballroom on Sherbrooke Street, across from the campus. The article no doubt contributed to the frenzy and assured that there would be a rush to attend the lecture.

In his article, entitled "Houdini is Sworn Enemy of All Mediums," Nelles humourously begins by asking Houdini "if he could say a few words. The master wizard and terror of fake mediums recites, with a twinkle in his eye, the whole alphabet from A to Z. … and wound up with a series of words, something like dog, rat, cat, hat, and fat."

Nelles describes Houdini growing more serious as the interview proceeded. As soon as his questions moved to Houdini's favourite topic, the cheating mediums,

> his keen eyes narrowed slightly with the right lid giving the slightest suspicion of a droop. He spoke earnestly and it became obvious that this was the subject nearest his heart. His genius as a man whom no lock ever made by human brain could permanently shackle was but a means to an end. To spend his life in the relentless pursuit of these "spiritual" criminals was his supreme desire. His whole attitude suggested this. A soul lit by one idea had kept him constantly on the track: writing in magazines, giving addresses to the public and lecturing to the staffs of civic police and detective agencies. The exposure of fraud is, with him, an obsession and his marvellous ability to reproduce by natural means any phenomenon created by a materialistic faker has made him the subject of the most intense fear and hatred by the criminal class.

Nelles ends his report, echoing the feelings of Conan Doyle, that, ironically,

> Houdini himself has some wonderful power, the depths of which no other human has ever plumbed. Personal contact naturally gives no clue to his ability to extricate himself from the strongest criminal bonds of Washington and Scotland Yard. He still remains as baffling

as ever and as mysterious as always. *But how does he do it?*

In 1986, sixty years after he interviewed Houdini, I found Gordon Nelles, "eighty-two and still going strong," living in Hudson, Quebec, west of Montreal. A retired economist who headed the Canadian Chamber of Commerce in Montreal, he recalled the team of editors and reporters working at the *Daily* at the time. (Among the names to be found on the masthead are Leon Edel, the celebrated biographer of Henry James; John Glassco, author of *Memoirs of Montparnasse*, Charles Peters who became publisher of the Montreal *Gazette*; Ted Harris, later managing editor of the Montreal *Herald*; and David Legate, long-time book critic of the Montreal *Star*.) In various newspaper reports published after Houdini's death—and one still sees Halloween rewrites using this premise—the author of the blows to Houdini's stomach is described as a *McGill Daily* reporter engaged in a friendly "sparring match" with the magician. It's hardly likely that any members of the *Daily* staff could have been involved. There's no indication, at least not from a perusal of the mastheads, that J. Gordon Whitehead worked on the *Daily*.

When I met Nelles he insisted, curiously, that Houdini had already received the blows when he interviewed him Monday afternoon, October 18. The Whitehead punching incident, as noted, took place four days later. Nelles recalled that Houdini had had a heat lamp beamed on his stomach as he reposed on a cot in the dressing room. "He looked not very well, pretty white, and his wife Beatrice was worried about him." Nelles said that Houdini told him that he had received a strong punch in the stomach that hadn't braced his muscles for. "Suddenly—bang!— he received the punch in his appendix."

But sixty years after meeting Houdini, could Nelles simply have been confused, having heard so much over the years that he just assumed that the conjurer had been belted before he conducted his interview? Or had Houdini in fact been tested by someone else other than J. Gordon Whitehead, the mysterious Friday visitor? Nelles recalled trying to look up the fellow who hit Houdini, and, good reporter that he was, "checking through student directories looking for his name after I heard about the incident, but like you say, he seemed to have disappeared."

Gordon Nelles, 1986.
As an enterprising 22-year-old student reporter, Gordon Nelles
interviewed Houdini in his theatre dressing room.
Photo by Don Bell

At five o'clock on the Tuesday Nelles' story appeared, Houdini arrived at McGill Union to deliver his lecture. The next day in an unbylined story, not by Nelles, the *Daily* described it as the largest crowd that ever packed the Ballroom. "Every inch of standing room was taken up, many having to stand halfway down the stairs or on ladders to hear the lecturer." As expected, Houdini conducted a virulent and scathing attack on spiritualism "and all the mediums who claimed occult powers," including Margery of Boston, whom Houdini called "the slickest medium alive today." The *Daily* reports,

He told his audience that he had been invited to her séances and on the first night, much to her chagrin, he detected the tricks she used when her husband, Dr. Crandon, accidentally turned on the light and he caught somebody manipulating for her.

"She changes her routine every night. She hands out applesauce to the investigators. I know this because I have walked through the apple orchards myself," Houdini scoffed merrily.

"It's the easiest thing in the world to become a medium. All you have to do is to lie and say that you see spirits … They are the meanest grafters on earth because they rob the poor and troubled … They take advantage of people torn by sorrow of losing a loved one, and for a dollar more or less pretend to get a message from the dear departed."

Houdini said he was not allowed to attend many of these meetings because they said, "Ha! Ha! Here comes a disturbing element." Yet he said he had "examined more mediums than anyone else in the world, and I have never been converted.

"When asked if I could do anything religious, I said that the only thing I could do was take up the collection."

Houdini paused, waiting for the laughter to subside.

"Folks who hear voices and see forms," he went on, "ought to consult their family physician immediately."

The Montreal *Star* wrote that, "The theologs, meds and infant psychologists in the Union Ballroom were unanimous in agreeing that if Houdini had not decided to be the master magician of the age, he might have rivalled Mark Twain as a humourist." His speech, the *Star* said, was "exceptionally funny."

Houdini informed the audience that he was well-versed in the tricks of the mediumistic trade because he himself as a callow youth had started out working in Kansas as a professional medium, travelling with a quack doctor "who was a philanthropist because he sold medicine worth a hundred dollars a bottle for one dollar, and threw in an entertainment with it.

"I conducted religious spiritualist meetings and brought back spirits of the dead … I told the people of the town more about themselves than they ever suspected themselves. The trick was simple. In the morning I visited the country churchyard accompanied by the sexton and the oldest inhabitant. I gleaned more about the community from them than if I had lived there my whole life. The next day two prominent businessmen came and offered me twenty-five dollars to leave town before I told any more.

"Mediums exchange information," Houdini went on, "like Bradstreet or Dun to compile the inside dope on their victims."

He ended the lecture with the bodeful refrain, now almost a determinate part of his repertoire, "If I should die tonight, the mediums would declare a national holiday."

After the lecture, students surged forward toward Houdini. Some of the stories that were published after his death said that he had been challenged—and punched—during or after the lecture at the McGill Union. For instance, the Montreal *Gazette* reported on November 1, the day after Houdini's death, that "a playful punch" was thrown by a McGill student at the lecture when Houdini commented on his stomach muscles and his ability to withstand hard blows "without personal injury."

There is a possibility of one "hit", the Pickleman Punch which we discuss below, that may have taken place after Houdini left the Ballroom and conferred with some students downstairs in the billiards room on his way out. But McGill professor of psychology, Dr. William D. Tait, who organized and chaired the meeting, vigorously denied all reports of any punch-ups taking place at the McGill Union.

Is it even true that Houdini sometimes invited individuals to test his flexed stomach muscles? Nowhere in the literature are there eyewitness accounts of Houdini offering this challenge, other than in Montreal in his final days. It wasn't part of his show, as some Houdini scholars mistakenly assume. In 1995 I found one of Houdini's assistants. Dorothy Young, a retired dancer and Broadway performer in her eighties, living in California, had worked in the wings with Houdini up until a few months before the fatal event. She confirmed during a phone conversation that Houdini never invited people onstage to heave punches at his midsection. In fact, all the time she was with him, she said, she had never seen anyone actually test his abdominal muscles, on or off the stage.

Many years after all this happened, I had a conversation with Ron Finegold, librarian at the Montreal Jewish Public Library where I was scanning microfilm of the *Canadian Jewish Chronicle* to see how they reported the death of Ehrich Weiss, aka Harry Houdini.

Finegold related that when he was a youngster his family doctor was Dr. Herman Warshaw, who during the 1920s had been unofficial house physician for vaudeville troupes performing in Montreal. A dapper downtown character who hung out around stage doors, he knew all the show people that passed through Montreal.

Finegold recalled asking the doctor if he knew Houdini or had seen him perform. Dr. Warshaw told him that he had treated Houdini after he was walloped, that he told the magician he was seriously injured and advised him to cancel his show and look after himself and not go on to Detroit.

I wondered if Dr. Warshaw had left any paper or diaries or medical files where the Houdini incident was mentioned. He died in 1969 at age seventy-nine. I managed to trace Leonard Warshaw, the son of Dr. Warshaw's wife Ruth from a previous marriage. "He treated many famous entertainers passing through Montreal," Leonard Warshaw confirmed. "He was a helluva doctor, but he kept everything in his head. He wasn't the type to keep files on patients, he just remembered. If Houdini had any secrets to tell him, he probably took them with him to the grave."

2

What Killed Harry Houdini?

∾

I PLACED LETTERS in newspapers and magazines and went on the radio soliciting anyone who had seen Houdini perform in Montreal or who had been at his lecture at McGill to step forward. It is curious that almost everyone who did gave a different account of the slugging episode: where it took place, who the students were, how many were involved, and what killed Houdini. The most frequent misconception, thanks to Hollywood's *Houdini* with Tony Curtis as the magic man, is that he died after being trussed up and locked inside a casket which was lowered into an underwater chamber from which he couldn't escape.

Montrealer Tilya Helfield's late aunt, Minnie Gallay, had recently graduated from McGill University Medical School and was interning at the Grace Hospital in Detroit. She was on duty when Houdini was brought in. "This is a sort of family legend," Tilya wrote. By coincidence, her father, Wilfred Gallay—Minnie's brother—a retired chemist living in Ottawa, was studying at McGill and had attended Houdini's Ballroom lecture.

After Tilya spoke to him about the project, Gallay plumbed his memory, writing a long, entertaining letter. He recalled that after Houdini had finished preaching against the "vicious chicanery" of the spirit mediums, "a clamour arose from some of the packed audience, both students and faculty members, for Houdini to do some of his tricks. For instance, he was asked if it was true that by an exercise of will he could stand any pain at all."

The magician, according to Wilfred Gallay, produced a long needle which was examined by the audience, "and calmly pierced his cheeks so that the needle made an entrance and an exit. He said he felt no pain."

Trick or yogic powers? Houdini performed this feat often, telling the audience it wasn't a trick, merely that he did not bleed easily. As for him being injured by an unexpected punch, Gallay said that the event took place in

> the evening, after the show, while Houdini was resting on a couch in his hotel room when he was visited by two McGill students. The students chatted with him for a few moments, and then asked him whether he could take any hard blow and not feel it. Houdini was tired and not feeling well, and was probably relaxed. Without warning, one of the boys delivered a hard blow with his fist to Houdini's abdomen, which elicited a wince.
>
> There is no doubt that Houdini had an appendicitis, and the blow caused a perforation. Peritonitis set in, and the doctors in Detroit, including my sister who had just completed her medical studies at McGill, were unable to save him. … The story of the fatal blow was told to me directly by one of the two students present whom I knew—but I have forgotten his name, nor would I remember it if I heard it again. The story of his treatment and death in Detroit was told to me directly by my sister.

Contrast his story with that of John D. Powell of the University of Guelph's Biological Sciences Department. He wrote that his uncle, Joseph Henry Roydon Scotland, late of La Scala, "where he was the leading basso profundo under the name of Giuseppe Scotti for seven years," was on a solo world tour, "and was sharing the bill with Harry Houdini in Montreal on the night of the attack."

Houdini in fact was not sharing the bill with other acts, but there was a full accompanying orchestra in the pit below the stage. Powell continues,

> My uncle told me he was in the dressing room with Mr. Harry Houdini when McGill students came in and asked if they could punch Mr. Houdini's tightened gut—this they did until he said, "That's enough," turning to talk to my uncle. As he was relaxed another McGill student struck hard into the now soft abdomen causing the fatal injury.

Like one of Houdini's illusions, many different images mirror his death.

As I would later discover, the students Smiley, Price, and Whitehead were alone in the dressing room with Houdini when he was socked in the stomach. The name of the soloist Scotti does not show up anywhere in Houdini literature, although maybe he was around then. Possibly every version of what happened has a grain of truth.

One thing is certain: Houdini died in Detroit on Halloween. Or is even that? Magicians still titter when they're together, conjecturing that if Houdini's coffin in the Machpelah Cemetery in Queen's, New York where he is "supposedly" buried were to be opened, it might be empty. His death is commemorated every Halloween as magicians and present-day mediums, now more respectably known as psychics, gather around a séance table somewhere in the United States or Canada, exhorting Houdini please to rise from the dead, please to return to us in this terrestrial humus just for a short how-de-do.

Newspapers, medical reports, and biographies tell us that Houdini died at Detroit's Grace Hospital at 1:26 p.m., October 31, 1926.

What killed him is still a source of medical controversy. Officially, the cause was peritonitis, which the *Oxford Medical Companion* defines as "inflammation of the peritoneum, usually resulting from the rupture of a hollow viscus such as the appendix." The peritoneum is the strong membrane that lines the abdomen and helps hold the appendix, the intestines, the bowels, the liver, and the other internal organs in place.

The facts, everyone agrees, are as follows: first, Houdini received the crunching blows in Montreal; almost immediately afterward, he experienced severe abdominal pain. Nevertheless, he completed his remaining shows, one on Friday night only a few hours after being punched, and then the matinée and evening shows Saturday, after which he left with Bess and his troupe on the overnight train for Detroit.

During the voyage, he was in terrible agony. But there was no time to rest. Sunday, October 24 he was scheduled to begin his two-week run at Detroit's Garrick Theatre. The tour had received plenty of advance press coverage and his opening night show was sold out. But Houdini had a fever of 104°F (40°C). Every gesture must have been torture. At the end of the long, demanding first act, he collapsed in the wings. He forced himself back on his feet, doggedly went on and, incredibly, completed the show, although his assistants had to finish some of his tricks for him.

Houdini returned to the Statler Hotel where he was examined by the young hotel physician on duty, Dr. Daniel Cohn. Aware that the magician was very sick, diagnosing the problem as acute appendicitis, he put through a call to the surgeon Dr. Charles S. Kennedy. They determined that he was extremely ill with appendicitis and it was urgent that he be admitted immediately to Grace Hospital. Houdini, proud to the last, demurred, and it wasn't until his family physician, Dr. William Stone, was reached in New York that he agreed to go in. At 3 a.m. Monday Houdini was rushed to Grace Hospital. On Monday afternoon he was operated on. But the poison had seeped into his blood. Streptococcus peritonitis was diagnosed. The hospital released a bulletin, because by now the press was onto the story, describing Houdini's condition as "grave". There were no miraculous antibiotic drugs in Houdini's day which, had they existed, could have saved his life.

A second operation was performed; the procedure consisted of an opening in the abdomen, then the outer surface of the bowels was cleansed to try to drain away the septic material that had accumulated. There were more medical bulletins as Houdini's hours ticked away. His condition was now "less than favourable." A new experimental serum was tried. There are no details on the serum. A fellow Houdini researcher and foul-play theorist, Norman Bigelow of Fitchburg, Massassachussets, tried in 1985 to track down Houdini's medical file but was told by Harper-Grace Hospitals that the file was among those that had been destroyed "several years ago … as a matter of routine."

Houdini fought to the last, even apparently dictating a letter dated October 30, on P.T. Barnum stationery. The letter was brought to my attention by the Houdini Historical Center in Appleton, Wisconsin. It is addressed to "My dear Thomas". No one has been able to establish who this Thomas is. It is a curious letter, considering Houdini's condition. Is it bona fide, or is there an error in the date? Houdini wrote, "Box offices here are S.R.O., which certainly makes me smug and quite happy. Except that I feel none too well at the moment, but suppose that I will get over this waviness in no time."

Waviness? It is beyond even a Houdini with his superhuman strength and will-power to escape the just-as-determined Grim Reaper. One can imagine Houdini's agony in the jaws of death. *Black's Medical Dictionary* gives a vivid description of the terminal phase of peritonitis. Houdini would have been recumbent on his back, knees drawn up and propped by a pillow beneath them, his hands resting on his head. His abdomen would have been distended and the muscles of which he was so proud would now have been rigid. "The slightest pressure or movement [causes] severe and sickening pain." His urine would have been scanty, highly coloured, and passed with difficulty. He would have had a scorching fever. His pulse would have been "small, hard, and wiry." Constipation, hiccoughs, and vomiting are part of the condition. In the final hours, his temperature would fall, his face would become pinched, cold, and clammy, and his pulse rapid and feeble.

"But the patient's mental faculties generally remain quite clear till the close," the medical dictionary tells us.

Halloween afternoon, Houdini whispered to his brother Theo at his bedside, "I'm tired of fighting, Dash. I guess this thing is going to get me."

He succumbed. The message was sent out on the wires, and the world grieved—everyone, we can assume, except a few grudge-bearing mediums. For now at last they would have their national holiday and dance the celebratory ectoplasmic cha-cha-cha on the streets.

The debate over what killed Harry Houdini—was it a natural peritonitis resulting from an ruptured inflamed appendix, or the result of the so-called "accidental" punch?—arose at once because of the double-indemnity accident insurance policy Houdini had out with New York Life, one of the four companies where he was insured, although he had only one double-indemnity policy. If his insurers could be convinced that his death was unquestionably accidental, that the blows he received were the result of "a playful student prank," Mrs. Houdini stood to gain an additional $25,000 under the double-liability clause, a handsome sum in 1927 when the claim was made. On the other hand, if it was shown that Houdini died of natural causes, or had been struck maliciously and intentionally—which never seemed to cross anyone's mind; there is no known police investigation—then it wasn't likely that she would smoothly collect another twenty-five grand.

Affidavits by the three students who were in Houdini's Princess Theatre dressing room were drawn up at Mrs. Houdini's behest, each giving his version of the story. Up to now, biographers seem to have overlooked these affidavits. My letters and phone calls to the New York law offices of Ernst, Cane, Gitlin and Winick, successors to Bernard Ernst's firm Ernst, Fox and Cane, and to all the insurance companies where Houdini had policies—Metropolitan, Fidelity Mutual, and Union Central as well as New York Life—did not unearth the affidavits. The insurance companies said their files going back that far had been destroyed or that nothing could be found in their vaults. The office of Paul Gitlin replied that a check had been made through the firm's storage vault, but "unfortunately, we find all files pertaining to [Houdini] have been lost."

The heart of the medical debate is whether a wallop, or wallops, to the stomach could cause appendicitis or aggravate a pre-existing appendicital condition. The consensus of the doctors was that although appendicitis provoked by such a trauma is a rarity, it was not unknown. Two of the doctors who treated Houdini even cited cases of people being kicked in the abdomen by a horse, which caused, declared one, "a very definite traumatism of the appendix." Modern medical experts, however, are of a different opinion. They will tell you that it's impossible for a "blunt trauma," as a non-piercing injury is known in medicalese, to directly cause appendicitis, but the contusion could provoke internal bleeding, and if the blood became infected, peritonitis could result.

I discussed Houdini's death with many doctors. My cousin Dr. Philip Belitsky, a surgeon and professor of urology at Dalhousie University in Halifax, Nova Scotia, suggested that the appendicitis might have been an entirely independent event, developing on its own:

It's hard to believe that appendicitis could have occurred as a result of the blow. But if you had a really severe blow, you could get a small tear in the bowel adjacent to the appendix or some place close by, through which blood and bacteria could escape into the peritoneal cavity. But the appendix would not likely be the structure that would be involved by that. Alternatively, it's possible that the offending micro-organisms gained entrance during the first operation, especially if the appendix had burst. It's when the abdominal wall becomes open, during surgery, for instance, or by leakage of bowel contents from injuries or infections that contamination can occur. Without Houdini's medical files though, it would be hard to make a correct diagnosis. The tenseness of his muscles most certainly could have had an influence. Muscles which are girded and tense would decrease the chance of serious injury.

Most doctors are at least agreed that if Houdini had serious abdominal problems, the stomach-smashes certainly wouldn't have made him feel any better. The five physicians who treated him were all of that opinion. Although they must have felt compassion for Mrs. Houdini, whom they came to know personally, it's hard to imagine that they would have dishonoured their Hippocratic oath for the sake of her double-indemnity financial security. Their conclusion was that there was a definite connection between the pounding Houdini received in Montreal and the peritonitis. Harry's demise was accepted as resulting from an accident by New York Life, and Bess, in mid-1927, collected the extra sum. We can say with reasonable certainty that the blows inflicted in Montreal, especially the attack at the Princess, directly or indirectly contributed to Houdini's death.

But was it an accident?

New York Life might have come to another conclusion if it had sent its investigators deeper into the trenches. If they had made further inquiries about the man with the trench coat and the hammer fists, and maybe some other incidents as well.

3

The Pickleman Punch

~

IN 1986, a few years after I started this research, the amiable Montreal magician Magic Tom Auburn gave me a tip. When he heard I was on the Houdini case, he suggested calling his former family doctor, Dr. Munro Bourne, who had retired to Rothesay, New Brunswick. He said that Dr. Bourne was around McGill at the time Houdini was punched and might know something about Whitehead.

Dr. Bourne's memory was hazy. He knew Houdini had received some kind of punch to the midriff, but the person who might really be able to help, he suggested, was Dr. William Cohen in Montreal.

Dr. Cohen said he was a student at McGill in 1926. He recalled that it was a fellow student, Gerald Pickleman, who he thought was connected with the *McGill Daily*, who punched Houdini, and it happened not in the Princess Theatre but at the McGill Union. He remembered Houdini speaking in the Union Ballroom about fraudulent mediums, vehemently attacking them, and performing a few tricks including piercing his jowls with a needle, as yogis did, without drawing blood. "When his cheeks were examined by McGill's dean of medicine," Dr. Cohen recalled, "there wasn't a single puncture mark where the needles went through." He couldn't remember much more—it was all too long ago. He suggested trying to trace Pickleman through McGill's Alumni Association.

The Association did, in fact, have a Gerald Pickleman in its computer, at a Fort Lauderdale address. It was easy enough to obtain his number from Florida information; I called and a woman with a friendly voice answered. She said that she was Mrs. Pickleman, but that her husband had died in 1981.

"What is it about?" Annette Pickleman asked.

When I explained, she readily confirmed that her husband had been with a group of students at the McGill Union and had accepted an invitation by Houdini to test his stomach muscles by punching him in the abdomen.

"Gerry told the story many times," she said. "whenever Houdini's name came up, but in later years people hadn't discussed it with him as much. It wasn't a thing he boasted about, but nor was it a secret or anything he ever tried to hide. He had the normal guilt a person would have. He was a sensitive man, not the kind of person who would go around punching people. He wasn't even aware [that a punch had caused Houdini's death] until after the autopsy. That's when he began to talk about it."

As for details of the event: "There was a needle involved, and there were other young men in the room with him … it's vague." After her husband passed away, Mrs. Pickleman said, she'd gone through his papers but had unfortunately thrown many things away, including scrapbooks with articles from what she thought was a student newspaper, in which her husband may have written about Houdini's show in Montreal.

I checked the *McGill Daily* files and no articles by Pickleman about Houdini could be found, and his name does not appear on the masthead in the fall of 1926.

"If Gerry mentioned the incident, it was usually at a gathering with friends. It was something he might have talked about back in the 1920s and 1930s and a few years afterwards, and occasionally as time went on he'd mention it, but Houdini's name didn't come up that often in latter years."

Pickleman's son Jack, a Chicago surgeon, later told me that he never heard his father speak of Houdini.

Annette Pickleman said she couldn't remember her husband ever mentioning Whitehead, Smiley, or Price. And Smiley had said he didn't recognize the name "Pickleman." It would seem the Whitehead incident and the Pickleman punch are not related, although if Whitehead was at Houdini's McGill lecture, he may very well have been in the audience when Pickleman tested Houdini's stomach muscles.

Pickleman went to medical school, but dropped out to join the Canadian Army Medical Corps. In 1933 he and Annette moved to

Watertown, New York, where her family had a furniture store. As it expanded into a seven-store chain, Gerry Pickelman worked there until 1964 when he sold his interest, although he remained active in business even after retiring to Florida.

Was he the boxer at McGill, or the football player, or the *McGill Daily* reporter referred to in Houdini biographies and newspaper reports? Mrs. Pickleman didn't recall her husband ever saying that he boxed at McGill. Football? "Yes, for a while, but he had to give that up when he broke his left elbow. That prevented him from participating in contact sports." The *Daily* reporter? Possibly. Dozens of students wrote for the paper, sometimes without bylines.

Pickleman may very well have been the McGill student some of the reporters had in mind when referring to the Houdini sparring match. He did, after all, test Houdini's stomach muscles with a punch, as he himself playfully told friends at parties, according to his wife. But it's doubtful that the Pickleman punch was anything more than a reply to a legitimate invitation. As Annette described him, he was the type "who probably would have been the first one to volunteer for something like that." It seems unlikely that he had any intention of harming Houdini.

In 1991 I would hear from a man named Jack Hausner who witnessed the Pickelman punch.

An 84-year-old Montrealer sunbirding in Palm Beach, Florida, Hausner replied to a letter planted in the Montreal *Gazette* asking for any old-timers who remembered Houdini's act in Montreal or who knew about him being slugged, to please step forward.

Hausner wrote that he had been a commerce undergraduate at McGill in 1926.

"I remember being in a group of people at the McGill Union when Houdini was giving an informal demonstration of his powers of escaping from a series of chains, shackles, ropes and gags and other such paraphernalia," he wrote.

I remember clearly his challenge to anyone in the group to punch him—with all his might!—in his stomach so that he could demonstrate his powers of concentration to withstand physical pain and survive unharmed.

I must differ with you concerning the identity of the person who delivered the blow which apparently resulted in his death a week or two later. That person was *not* Gordon Whitehead, as you believe. If my memory serves me correctly, it was an undergraduate well known to many of us at the time, name GERALD PICKLEMAN (or PICKELMAN). … He came from a family who lived in upper New York State. … I trust I haven't sent you an on unnecessary wild goose chase, but in the interests of accuracy … I believe it's worth the trouble.

When Hausner returned to Montreal, we talked over the phone, and he had some further recall about the Pickleman affair. The actual punching event took place at an informal gathering at the McGill Union, he said, with only about a dozen students present.

"It was in a public room where students went to socialize—to shoot a game of pool or snooker. Houdini was passing through and we engaged him in conversation. He was very warm when we met him.

"Pickleman was a pretty burly fellow, but as far as I knew he wasn't a boxer and didn't work for the *McGill Daily*, although anyone could have contributed an article from time to time. Houdini had time to prepare himself. The blow wasn't unexpected. Pickleman was 170 pounds or so, five feet seven or nine. It was just one blow."

Hausner knew Smiley, but didn't recall him being at the gathering. The names Price and Whitehead didn't mean anything to him.

If his story is correct, and it seems to be since it backs up Annette Pickelman's account, it contradicts the well-publicized statement by Dr. William Tait of McGill's psychology department, who had invited Houdini to give the lecture. Dr. Tait was quoted in the Montreal *Star* on November 1, 1926:

When Houdini completed his address, he sat down immediately [on one of two chairs on the platform] as he was suffering great pain from his fractured ankle. Certain members of the faculty and students came up and shook hands with Houdini as he sat there. His nurse came up to the platform and insisted upon Houdini leaving so a pathway was made for him. He got out of the hall quickly and was hurried away in his waiting taxi. There was no opportunity for a sparring match, friendly or otherwise.

Tait may have been concerned about the university's good name, or not aware of the challenge in the public room downstairs reported by Jack Hausner and Annette Pickleman.

But wait, there is more to come! … Houdini got belted again.

4

Attack at the Prince

∽

WHEN HOUDINI performed in Montreal, he stayed at the Prince of Wales Hotel on McGill College Avenue near Ste. Catherine, just a few blocks west of the Princess Theatre. The fifty-two-room hotel, torn down after World War II, was a home away from home for many of the vaudeville performers when they played the city. It was full even when the larger downtown hotels like the Mount Royal, Windsor, and Queen's had vacancies on every floor. The hotel had a fancy restaurant with a topflight chef, live dinner music, and a popular "plate lunch" buffet for sixty cents which owner Francis Larin introduced in the 1920s. In had one of the busiest taverns in the city, the Pig & Whistle, a favourite watering hole for McGill students.

I first heard about the Prince of Wales attack in a 1990 letter from Gilles Larin, a Montreal human resources consultant and grandson of the owner. He wrote that his grandfather had bought the hotel, known then as the Welland, in 1919 and renamed it the Prince of Wales in tribute to the prince's visit to Montreal that year. Francis Larin had been a musician, a member of John Philip Sousa's military band, and, according to his grandson, knew Houdini well and was friendly with most of Houdini's orchestra and the members of his troupe, who stayed at the hotel.

The story of Houdini being slugged in the Prince of Wales lobby has always been part of the Larin family lore, Gilles wrote. He remembered hearing it from his grandfather when he was a child, and also from his father.

He postulated in the letter that the Whitehead attack was the "so-called official version," but this better known pummelling in his grandfather's hotel could have caused as much damage to Houdini as the other blows he received in Montreal and very likely contributed to his demise. Larin related:

> After giving a performance Houdini usually had a meal and relaxed in the Prince of Wales lobby, reading newspapers. In the back of the hotel was a tavern frequented by McGill students. It had a door leading to the lobby, but when the hotel closed at 11 p.m., the students usually went out through the rear exit leading to the lane in back.
>
> But that particular night when Houdini was there waiting to board the overnight train that would take him and his company to Toronto, Buffalo, etc. and then to Detroit, three or four students who were rather drunk spilled out of the tavern into the lobby. One of them, mimicking the act that Houdini presented in his show where he dared anyone to hit him in the stomach [although Houdini was noted for this challenge, it was not part of his performance on stage], walked up to Houdini, who was sitting in a lounge chair reading a newspaper, and, without any warning, hit him through the news-paper, in the stomach, a crunching blow. Houdini, doubled over in pain, said, "You shouldn't have done that," then got up, very slowly, and walked out of the lobby.

The attack, Gilles elaborated when we met in a restaurant a few days later, was in fact not witnessed by his grandfather, but by Francis' brother Honoré, the night clerk who was in the lobby just ten feet away from Houdini. Two other hotel clerks and a bellboy also witnessed the assault. His grandfather found out about it only the next morning. Houdini of course by then had already left on the train for Detroit.

We decided to drive up to visit Gilles' father Marcel, in his late seventies. An "eclectic inventor," as his son described him, Marcel was known as the designer of taxi dome lights and of various electronic and radio devices used by the U.S. Navy during the Second World War. Widowed, he lived in a duplex in Montreal's north end and still puttered around in a workshop garage full of electronic gadgets.

Marcel said he was strongly influenced by Houdini, so much so that for a while in his younger days he enthusiastically took up magic himself. It was in no small part due to Houdini, who symbolized for him humankind's capacity to realize the dreams of the imagination and perform the impossible, that he became an inventor.

Because of Marcel's passion for magic, in 1926 his father used his influence with Houdini and the musicians to get him and his brother Rodolphe admitted backstage and into the orchestra pit to wit-ness Houdini's magic up close.

"I remember passing under the stage and seeing the apparatus Houdini had and the trapdoors which he used with the help of accom-plices to escape from caskets and all manner of sealed containers. It was an incredible experience for a boy who loved magic."

Marcel heard about the Prince of Wales incident from his father and his Uncle Honoré. It was much the same story told by his son: the students lingering in the lobby after the Pig & Whistle closed, one of them who was "burly like a football player" approaching Houdini as if having premeditatively chosen him as his quarry, and suddenly swinging at him through the newspaper; Houdini doubling up in pain, then lifting himself up saying, "You should not have done that without warning," and shakily making his way to the hotel office.

"And a few days later," Marcel said, "good night, Houdini."

He didn't think a report was ever filed with the police, although the punch was "much discussed" by his father and uncle and hotel staff after Houdini died, especially when the autopsy report concluded that an abdominal blow was the cause of the magician's death. He was always moved and saddened, he said, whenever his father showed him the lounge chair where Houdini sat reading his newspaper when the attack took place.

Could these "students" have been henchmen hired by Houdini's enemies, as Whitehead too may have been, to deliver the message of a spiritualist balancing of accounts?

5

How Far Would They Go?

YEARS BEFORE his death Houdini told his boyhood friend Joseph Rinn, "Those mediums are bad actors and would think nothing of putting you in the hospital or worse."

Houdini saw them not only as tricksters and scoundrels, but also would-be criminals who would go to any lengths to fend off adversaries like himself who would dare to hinder them from milking unwary clients for lucrative ends.

One need look no further than his own book *Houdini—A Magician Among the Spirits* to catch an idea of how far these so-called ambassadors from otherworldly realms who had liaison with "departed souls" would go:

> During the more than thirty years in which I have been investigating Spiritualism, I have industriously collected all possible data on the subject and in the thousands of clippings, dating from 1854 to the present time filed away in my library, there are hundreds which tell of crimes attributable to Spiritualism.

He cites, for example, Charles J. Guiteau, the assassin of President Garfield:

> It is not generally known that he was a pronounced Spiritualist. He claimed that he was inspired by the Spirits four times. Once in connection with his entering the Oneida community. Once preceding his attempt to establish a newspaper called *The Theocrat*. Again when writing his book *The Truth: A Companion to the Bible*,

and still again when he was inspired to kill the President.

In the chapter "How Mediums Obtain Information" Houdini shows how these "swindlers" connived and conspired to gather information, often obscure tidbits, about their clientele to use during séances:

I am familiar with a great many of the methods of these human vultures. I think though it is an insult to that scavenger of scavengers to compare such human beings to him, but there is, to my mind, no other fit comparison.

Their stock-in-trade is the amount of knowledge they can obtain. It is invaluable and they will stop at nothing to gain it.

They will tabulate the death notices in the newspapers; index the births and follow up the engagement and marriage notices. … They will hunt through the court records of property and mortgages … and employ young men to attend social affairs and mix intimately with the guests, particularly the women.

He knew of mediums who hired burglars to break into the apartments of clients "not to steal valuables, but information which yields them far more than the small amount of diamonds and cash which they might snatch."

Many had insiders working for them in post offices, restaurants, beauty parlours, even Turkish baths. "While the patrons were enjoying the bath their clothes were searched, letters opened and signatures traced." He continues:

The most dastardly and unscrupulous methods that I ever heard of, methods almost beyond belief, were those used by a medium who made arrangements with a ring of "white slavers" by which he paid them a certain specified sum for any information which the "girls" in their "houses" were able to secure.

Most of the mediums work in the dark, and many of them have employed expert pickpockets who cleverly take from the sitters' pockets letters, names, memorandums, etc. while they are being interviewed. These are passed to the medium who tells the sitter more or less of their contents. Having served their purpose they are returned to the pockets of the sitter who, none the wiser, goes out to help spread reports of the medium's wonderful ability.

I have known of a number of cases in which the medium used a drug addict to secure information, giving the poor tortured creature his necessary drug only in return for facts he wanted, knowing that when the addict was suffering for the drug's stimulus he would stop at nothing to secure it.

We have prohibition of alcohol, we have prohibition of drugs, but we have no law to prevent these human leeches from sucking every bit of reason and common sense from their victim.

Fighting words that provoked the conjurors of ectoplasmic entities. Houdini revelled each time he caught one of them up to dirty tricks and, pleased with himself, would expose them to ridicule in his pamphlets and books, or on stage.

The point is: if the mediums would go to such extremes to fleece their clientele, often rich elderly ladies with high social standing, distraught after having lost a husband or a relative, then it seems natural to imagine that if their livelihood was threatened they would arrange some skulduggery, hiring or convincing a person crazy enough to believe in spirits, to weasel his way into Houdini's confidence, to trick the trickster, and then let him have it when his guard was down.

Let's review some of the suspects.

First, Margery of Boston, the witch of Beacon Hill whose séances Houdini exposed with abandon. Obviously she didn't throw any punches at Houdini, and probably wasn't even in Montreal when he was pummelled, but she did predict his death and threatened him through her spirit guide Walter.

Norman Bigelow, one of the foremost foul-play theorists, postulates in his 1983 booklet *Death Blow*,

If Houdini truly did die as a result of the punches, then the question of murder is a fine line. It depends what was in the student's mind at the time. ... Did he plan to do it? Did mediums send him to do it? Was he angry about Houdini's answers on the Bible? Did he lose his temper on the spot? Certainly a person could be murdered in this fashion and then have it called an accident by an expert.

The gathering of suspects might include James P. Clarke, who wrote to Conan Doyle with unreserved hostility toward Houdini the day before Houdini was attacked. If Sherlock Holmes had been on the case, he might have investigated further, for instance comparing Clarke's handwriting to Whitehead's.

The suspects might include Mrs. Cecil Cook, the New York City medium who made trumpets float about the room during her séances and had the spirits of the departed ones take possession of her vocal organs so that they might talk to the sitters. Houdini went to one of the Trumpet Medium's séances disguised as an old man. She paid special attention to the refined elderly client who seemed rather rich, seating him at the table close to her. The lights were turned out and soon the voice of a boy came through the trumpet.

"Hello, Dad. Don't you know me?"

Mrs. Cook told the old man that the message was for him and that he should speak to the spirit.

Houdini said, "Good evening, kind spirit."

The boyish voice continued, "Don't you know me, Dad? This is your son, Alfred."

"Surely not my son Alfred?" queried Houdini.

The spirit assured him that such was the case, which of course was a true miracle, bringing back the dead son of Houdini, for he had never been so blessed.

In the darkened room was a New York policewoman. As the voice of Houdini's supposed son came through the trumpet, the lights were turned on and there sat Mrs. Cook with the trumpet to her lips. Houdini threw off his disguise; the medium lay on the floor in an alleged faint from the effects of the light being thrown upon her while in a trance. A rush was made at the now at-bay "old man", who displayed his police badge, Houdini being a reserve member of the New York Police Department. The very name "Houdini" brought the medium to her feet. She was arrested, found guilty, and fined $100.

Some months later, her mentor, who wished to "wipe clean the slate of my past", said in a sworn statement that she had taught the Trumpet Medium all the tricks she knew and had sent her a stream of clients—bankers, lawyers, chiefs of police. She explained that she had promised her mother on her deathbed that she would give up her work and make amends. Thus she went to Houdini. The Trumpet Medium's teacher said that since she started to expose her colleagues, "I have been threatened time and again that my life would be in danger if I did not stop."

Mrs. Cook also had to retire.

Houdini opposed and exposed others who had motive enough to hate him and harm him. Pierre O.L. Keeler was the dean of slate-writers; when Houdini trapped him red-handed he confessed that he was guilty of fraud and pleaded to be let off lightly when he was about to be arrested. Minnie Reichart from Chicago was another trumpet medium whom Houdini exposed by taking a flashlight photo showing her in action. He made several spiritualists appear ridiculous in a public investigation in Washington just a few months before the punching incident in Montreal.

There was John Slater, the millionaire medium who had a reputation as the cleverest message-reader in spiritism. On June 23, 1926 Houdini crashed a meeting of the Pennsylvania State Spiritualist Association at the Lu Lu Temple in Philadelphia, ready to expose Slater's trickery and subterfuge and offering to donate $10,000 to charity if Slater would read five messages that he, Houdini, had sealed in envelopes. Forewarned that Houdini would be at the meeting, Slater hid.

"After the meeting," reported the *Philadelphia Record* the next day,

> a brawl occurred on the pavement outside the Lu Lu Temple. Women engaged in fistfights, and cries of "Fraud!" and "Cheat!" were directed against both Slater and Houdini. The millionaire medium kept within the inner recesses of the building. ... The crowd gathered around the automobile of Rev. Mary H.M. Ellis, who was conveying Houdini downtown. They jeered and there were loud cries. The spiritualists were frantic.

Mediums galore stood to benefit if Houdini was out of the picture. As Norman Bigelow wrote, "The theory of murder was not nonsense to Houdini or many other people in those days. Houdini, himself, felt he would be killed and that fraudulent mediums would do it."

In many of his letters and conversations, in fact, Houdini made it clear that he thought he was on the spiritualists' hit list; that probably he didn't have long to live. In *Arthur Ford: The Man Who Talked with the Dead* by Allen Spragget with William V. Rauscher, Houdini is quoted as telling the novelist Fulton Oursler, " 'Probably I'm talking to you for the last time; they are going to kill me.' 'Who?' asked Oursler. Houdini replies, 'Fraudulent spirit mediums.'"

Conan Doyle showed no surprise over Houdini's death. He seemed to know something was up. In a letter sent some years later to Harold Kellock, one of Houdini's biographers, he states, "In my private circle at my home in March [1926], my wife, under spirit influence, wrote, 'Houdini is Doomed, Doomed, Doomed!'"

In other words, writes Bigelow, "the spirit revealed to them Houdini's nearing fate before it happened. It was not a great secret. A lot of people knew Houdini was going to die and those that know the truth know that it was not the work of the Lord. When the final truth comes out, it will prove all of Houdini's claims that mediums will commit any act to stay in business, even MURDER."

That Houdini survived two years after Margery's guide Walter gave him "a year or less" is itself amazing. But Houdini continued on strong to the end, ignoring the threats and defying his enemies. "While I have breath and ingenuity, both will be used to unmask preying fakirs, fortune tellers, diabolists and spirit mongers."

6

"I Certainly Didn't Like Him"

AMONG THE STUDENTS who attended Houdini's lecture in the jam-packed McGill Union Ballroom was Sam Smilovitz, a second-year arts undergraduate and keen amateur artist. Sam Smiley, as he was known later on, would become a Montreal corporation lawyer. He always carried a sketchpad with him. As he listened to Houdini, he was busily scratching the magician's portrait. At the end of the lecture, upon prompting from his fraternity brothers, Smiley showed Houdini the sketch. Impressed, Houdini invited him to do another drawing of him in his dressing room on Friday morning. Smiley's friend Jacques Price was also at the lecture, and without a doubt so was J. Gordon Whitehead, who was not known then to either Smiley or Price.

Sam Smiley is the source of the Princess Theatre dressing room story. Although his version of the incident was apparently given in an affidavit drawn up in 1927 (I say "apparently" because his and Jacques Price's and Whitehead's affidavits were proving elusive) it received wide play only after he was interviewed by Stanley Handman for a feature on Houdini's death that appeared in *Weekend Magazine* on September 12, 1953.

Before Handman's article, the incident had been mentioned fuzzily, and for the most part inaccurately, in Houdini biographies and articles, with the names of the students not given and the provenance of the story not clear. Often two students rather than three were placed in the dressing room, and invariably one was described as a member of McGill's boxing team. Handman's well researched article gave the names of the students and has been the basic source for most descriptions of the event that have appeared since then in newspapers and magazines and in the clutch of Houdini biographies—each new study seeming to siphon material from the previous. A similar version to Handman's, for instance, is found in Milbourne Christopher's 1969 book. It's not clear if Christopher interviewed Smiley or simply reworked Handman's material. A version of Smiley's story can be found in the Amazing Randi and Bert Sugar's illustrated large-format book *Houdini: His Life and Art*. That is where I first read about the dressing-room incident and what prompted me to phone Sam Smiley in October 1982. He was listed in the Montreal telephone directory. I asked him if he'd be willing to go through the story once more.

Our meeting took place in his cubby-hole office on the third floor of a four-storey office block, originally the Medico-Dental Building, at 1396 Ste. Catherine Street West (near Bishop), about ten blocks west of the Princess Theatre.

Unlike Whitehead, who was never publicly heard from again, or Jacques Price, Smiley has only been a phone call away from anyone with good enough reason for wanting to hear his ringside account of the fisticuffs in Houdini's dressing room.

Samuel J. Smiley was born in Quebec City in 1906, went to high school there, and entered McGill's Arts Faculty on a scholarship in 1923. He worked on the *McGill Daily* as a reporter, he was on the crew of the McGill Rowing Club, and apparently (I found this out only years later when speaking to his son Charles, a Montreal lawyer and film producer), he also did some boxing, although this was in Quebec City, not at McGill. It's unlikely that the McGill boxer referred to in some newspaper accounts of the dressing room episode was Sam Smiley, although there might have been some confusion if Smiley had told inquirers that he had once boxed. At McGill, rowing was the only sport he participated in. Charles Smiley said he could not remember his father being particularly athletic. "His passion has always been sketching and painting."

Seventy-six at the time of our first interview, Smiley lounged on a plush swivel chair behind a not particularly tidy oak desk that dominated his law office. His name suits him well. Many of the shopkeepers near his office, such as Jack and Frances Rodick who ran Rodick's second-hand bookstore on Ste. Catherine Street and who knew Whitehead and will be heard from later, always assumed that "Smiley" was a nickname bestowed on him because of his jovial demeanour. "He was always smiling and joking," Jack Rodick remembered.

"Fellow shows up at the door of this old Jewish couple," Smiley burst out within a few minutes of stepping into his office when I mentioned some research postulating that Jack the Ripper was a former McGill student, "and he shouts out at the top of his lungs, 'OPEN THE DOOR. I AM THE BOSTON STRANGLER!' Old Jewish guy opens the door, lets him in, tells him to hold on a moment, and hollers out to his wife, 'Betty! It's for you!'"

Sam Smiley rocked on his chair with peals of laughter, which would be repeated over the next few years whenever Jack the Ripper research was brought up, and invariably reminded him of the Boston strangler story.

Round-face, with lush eyebrows with twirly grey spikes sticking out of them, and great big jowls, Smiley had a raffishly Runyonesque aura. In his conservative grey suit and waistcoat he looked more like a judge relaxing in his chambers after a tough day on the bench than a mere corporate lawyer.

Before Houdini's name came up, Sam had his pencil and sketchpad out and was sketching away. "You look a lot like Augustus John," he said, although in this dinky film-noir setting I felt more like Sam Spade starting out on a new case.

On the walls hung several of Smiley's landscapes and portraits. He has always been quick, and proud, to mention, whenever he's asked about his painting career, the first prizes for brushstroke that he won at the École des Beaux Arts both in Montreal and Quebec City. (Even when I saw him at age eighty-eight, both legs amputated and residing in a care centre, he would still be passionately sketching away.) He told me his story while his pencil flew across the pad.

SMILEY'S STORY

I was an Arts student then at McGill, honouring in economics and history. Since I had some spare time, I was attending a psychology course given by Dr. William Tait, head of the psychology department.

Sam Smiley, 1982. Houdini invited university student Sam Smiley to
sketch him in his dressing room after a lecture he gave at
McGill University, Montreal.
Photo by Don Bell

It was Dr. Tait, in fact, who had organized Houdini's visit to McGill and he advised us to attend the lecture, saying that we would probably find it quite informative.

There were a few hundred students in the McGill Union Ballroom, all standing and pushing to get as close to Houdini on the podium as we could. I remember Houdini beginning his lecture by unleashing a fierce attack on the fake spiritualists, showing how they did their tricks and telling us it was all a lot of bunk and explaining how he went about unmasking them.

The lecture must have lasted about an hour and a half. I remember he did a little stunt putting a needle through his cheeks that greatly impressed everyone in the audience.

As I was a budding artist then, no sooner did he start talking than I had a pad out and began sketching him. How did he look? Not that healthy. No red cheeks, a sallow complexion. When the lecture ended, the Vim and Vigour fraternity brothers, whose house I was living in, said, "We're going to get him to autograph this." They went up to Houdini as he was leaving and showed him the drawing. Houdini cheerfully said, yes, he would autograph it, but only on one condition, that I be there [in the dressing room] on Friday morning to do another portrait of him, one just for himself.

I went to the theatre with a friend, Jacques Price, a student perhaps a little younger than myself, a nice fellow, but a nervous sort of boy. He was from England. Houdini's wife was there when we first went in, a cute little woman, but then she left. Houdini mentioned that he never has anyone with him alone so that he should not be misquoted, but with my friend Jacques Price and myself he'd make an exception.

So just the three of us were in there. His room was just a little bit bigger than this desk. While I was sketching him, he told us that his father was a rabbi, and his original name was Weiss. He said he got the name "Houdini" from a French magician of the day whom he admired, by the name of "Houdin". He told us that he tried Harry Houdini and it went like wildfire and he made a terrific success with that name.

While I was sketching him, he said, "Do you mind if I look through my mail? And I have to be reclining because I had a mishap while performing a trick last week in Albany, New York. I'm not in the best of shape but it's not visible on the stage."

[In the 1953 interview with Handman, Smiley had described Houdini's "tightly drawn skin … dark shadows encircling his tired-looking deep-set eyes. … The muscles about the temples and at the sides of his mouth twitched nervously, his mouth and eyes were tense."]

While I was drawing him, in comes this Gordon Whitehead, a fellow about forty or thereabouts. [Whitehead was actually thirty-one.] He was tall, at least six feet, smooth-shaven, almost bald, wearing a beige gabardine raincoat, and he was a divinity student, of all things. A student still at forty! He seemed brash and arrogant and I didn't like the intrusion at all. I didn't draw then as rapidly as I do now. He had a slight English accent and kept asking Houdini questions. He seemed to know him and was returning a book that he had apparently borrowed.

He said that as a divinity student he was curious if Houdini had any opinions about the miracles in the Bible. The question seemed to annoy Houdini. "I don't discuss these matters," he told Whitehead. But then he said, "I leave you boys with one thought: suppose I had been performing my magic in those days?"

And then Whitehead said, "Mr. Houdini, I hear you can resist blows struck to the abdomen." Houdini wasn't so proud of his abdominal muscles. He told us, "My back and forearm muscles are like steel." We felt his arm and it was like steel. And then Whitehead pops the question, "Would you mind if I struck a few blows to your abdomen?" I suppose it was his professional pride. Houdini says, "Go ahead."

He was reclining on the couch, propped up on pillows. He appeared to brace himself, but Whitehead didn't waste any time. He bends over—he was tall, lanky—and delivers a few direct blows to the abdomen, a good four or five. I just sat there, mouth agape, not knowing what was happening. I thought the whole thing was just some lunatic performance. But my friend Jacques Price had more presence of mind than I. He grabs hold of Whitehead and shouts, "Are you crazy or something?" and pulls him off Houdini. Houdini says, "That will do. Stop there."

Whitehead says a few words and then leaves, and I finish the sketch. And Houdini says, "Will you sign it?" I say, "Certainly." And I sign it, "S.J. Smilovitz, Arts/27". And Houdini says, "You'll be hearing from me."

[In the 1953 interview Smiley remembered Houdini telling him, "You make me look a little tired in this picture. The truth is that I do not feel very well."]

That was on the Friday morning. At any rate, a few days later there's a screaming headline in the paper: "Detroit Surgeons Say McGill Student's Blows Fell Houdini". Well, I didn't sleep that night, nor a number of nights after as he hovered between life and death—for five or six days I think, and he finally succumbed.

A month or so later they tell me there's a letter for me in the dean's office. It's from Ernst, Fox and Cane, the New York attorneys. They said, we understand you and your friends were in Houdini's room, and one of your friends struck the blows, and so forth, we understand it was purely accidental. Our sole interest is in collecting on a double indemnity accident insurance policy for Mrs. Houdini. Would you help by telling us what happened?

I showed the letter to Harry Cohen, a lawyer who was living at the Sigma Alpha Mu fraternity house with us on Shuter [now Aylmer] Street. He said I should write it right down. I did. But I said, before recounting what occurred I want to make two observations: there were three persons in the room when the blows were struck, and the blows were struck by the third person, not by my friend or myself. The New York attorneys wanted to put it into affidavit form and I recommended Harry Cohen and he was very grateful.

And he gets in touch with this fellow Whitehead. Now Harry

Cohen had had a peritonitis operation himself and he had this band around his waist and some of the bad matter was still oozing out of the wound. He tells me that when Whitehead came in for the affidavit, he was very arrogant and laughed about the incident, not in the least penitent. "Oh, it was nothing at all," he says to him, "let me show you how I did it." "No, no, don't show me," Cohen tells him. He thought Whitehead might be crazy enough to punch him in the abdomen like he did to Houdini.

I don't know what happened to Whitehead. I never saw or heard of him after the incident and moreover never wanted to. Why not? Because I thought he was crazy. I had no respect for fellows who were still going to college in their forties. I wasn't interested in knowing more about him. I regarded him as a crackpot. I didn't like the intrusion or the impertinent questions he asked, and I was terribly annoyed at him for having hurt Houdini, whom I admired very much. Not just his physical prowess, but I admired his mind. Even now I can recall Houdini's eyes as I drew him, sharp and piercing, penetrating. He had a superior intelligence, no question about that.

Did Smiley think it was possible that Whitehead was in collusion with the spiritualists? Sam Smiley leaned back, put his pencil down, studied the sketch he'd just completed of "Augustus John," fifty-six years after he likewise captured Houdini.

"I wouldn't know. I certainly didn't like him."

7

Steadfast

～

SINCE SAM SMILEY was the one and only source of the dressing room story, it seemed vital to draw out as many details from him as possible. He has been indisputably steadfast over the years. It's a trait that no doubt was already implanted when Smiley was at McGill. The inscriptions beside his graduation photo in the *Old McGill* yearbook for 1927, reads in his own words: "One cannot rest except after steady practice." And steadily he worked at his private law practice in Montreal from 1947 onward, after a brief flirtation with provincial politics. His secretary and girl Friday, Eva Fieldman, who had been with him for fifteen years, described her amiable boss as being even-tempered. His daughter, Karen, living on the Maine coast, said that her father "always had a good attitude toward life,"

This trait is crucial regarding the Houdini story. There would be several meetings with Smiley over the next few years and I phoned him from time to time. But his description of what happened remained fundamentally the same. A little detail may have been added because the question wasn't asked earlier, or some other detail forgotten if he wasn't pressed about a certain point. But the core of his story—Smiley would chortle every time he reported Houdini's answer to the question about Biblical miracles, "Can you imagine if I had been around then performing my tricks?"—has always been the same. There's never been any reason to question Smiley's credibility, or his memory, which even in his eighties seemed sharp.

In 1986, for instance, after having at last had some luck finding out who Whitehead was and what had happened to him, I was back in Smiley's office. He was eighty now ("A spring chicken," he chuckled) and still running his small corporation law practice, with Eva Fieldman minding the door. When I phoned to set up the appointment, I had asked again if he was sure that he had never met Whitehead after the Houdini punch. Smiley said, as he had during the earlier interview, that he had never seen him on the campus before or after the episode, that his only encounter with Whitehead, ever, was in Houdini's dressing room. He repeated the story told to him by his friend Harry Cohen about Whitehead offering to show him how he had sucker-punched Houdini.

"He was a crackpot," Smiley said over the phone, as he had during our first interview. "He boasted that he had hit Houdini. He bragged about it. He didn't show any great remorse."

We met a few days later. I asked him if we could go over some points that were crucial in trying to determine what Whitehead's intentions had been when he "tested" Houdini. Though arrogance alone does not make a murder suspect, by now I was becoming more and more convinced, especially after looking into the vendetta between the spiritualists and the magician and learning how Whitehead had so conveniently vanished, that there was something fishy about the whole episode. Even if Whitehead had not been officially hired, although this had not been ruled out, it still seemed as if he had a score to settle with Houdini.

And so it seemed necessary to plumb Smiley's memory as far as it could be plumbed. Could he, for instance, further describe Whitehead physically?

Smiley used the terms "raw-boned" and "lanky." "He towered over Houdini," he recalled. (I would later discover that Whitehead was six-foot two, and extremely powerful.) Smiley acknowledged that Houdini didn't flat-out refuse when Whitehead offered to test him. "He was awaiting the punch." This, of course, contradicts the popular notion that Houdini hadn't braced himself and was caught off guard. Once again Smiley pointed out that Houdini was reclining on his chair, propped up on pillows—an unusual position to be in if he was about to absorb a blow, but perhaps Houdini was so confident of his ability to knot up his muscles and resist such a blow that it didn't matter to him whether he was upright or reclined.

"How many blows?" I asked Smiley again. Surely one punch would have been enough for Houdini to prove his point and for the student to be satisfied. But Whitehead didn't back off. Smiley said now, as he had the first time, that four or five blows were delivered, and there was no pause between the punches. "They came in rapid succession."

Did Whitehead appear malicious or angry when he struck Houdini? Did he grimace? Did he clench his teeth? Did he seem resolved? Were his eyes ablaze? Did he say anything? If only he'd been captured on video.

"I looked upon him as a fool," was about as far as Smiley would go. "I still can't conceive of anybody being so idiotic."

Smiley said that the affidavits—his, Whitehead's, and probably one from Price—were sent to Ernst, Fox and Cane.

The subject of these lost affidavits was a delicate one. A California Houdini collector, Manny Weltman, reported to me that he had a letter which Smiley sent to Mrs. Houdini in 1927, "thanking her for sending him $100 for his affidavit." The first thought that came to mind when Weltman related this story, and he himself seemed to imply it, was that Smiley, a struggling young student at the time, might have been "tipped" by Mrs. Houdini to, well, who knows what?

So I finally brought up the subject.

"It was $200," Smiley corrected, not the least embarrassed. "It was for my helpfulness in collecting under the double-indemnity clause. When they asked me what I wanted, I told Mrs. Houdini 'Nothing'. And she sent me the $200. And, oh yes, she thought it was very nice that I didn't ask for anything."

His readiness and ease to explain the fee, even emphasizing that it was $200, not $100, seemed to overrule any suggestion that the story had been embellished or dictated to him.

In 1990, Smiley, now widowed, had an aorta bypass operation, and in 1991, because of blood circulation problems, his left foot became gangrenous and the leg had to be amputated above the knee.

He no longer had his office but I had been keeping in touch with Eva Fieldman. She said he was a patient in the geriatric unit of the Royal Victoria Hospital and no doubt would appreciate a visit.

I expected the worst when I dropped in on him in the spring of

1991, but other than the inconvenience of having lost a leg, he seemed as spry and cheerful as ever, a ready smile stretching across his round face. And still full of jokes, mostly of a medical nature: "I've been here for eleven months while the infection travelled all the way from Vancouver to Halifax.

"The doctors filled me with antibiotics," he continued as the nurse helped him out of the bed and onto a wheelchair. "They said they wanted to treat the infection from the inside. I said, 'Why don't you treat it from the outside?' After eleven months my foot had turned gangrenous and was as black as a piece of coal. They said, 'You have a choice. It's either your leg or your life.' Well, it wasn't hard to decide."

I showed Smiley a photo that had been found of Whitehead. Yes, he was quite sure that was him. But there wasn't much more to ask or for him to tell about Houdini. We had pretty much covered the event from all angles.

"Did you hear about the opera singer?" Smiley asked when I mentioned I'd be leaving soon for France. "She went to Paris for five years because she didn't want to be a virtuoso any more." Racked with laughter, he almost tumbled off the wheelchair.

Three years went by. In December 1994, having made inroads tracing Whitehead and Jacques Price, and having started the actual writing of this book, I looked up Sam Smiley again. The man who was there when Houdini was clouted—by now I was sure, deliberately—was now eighty-eight and residing in a long-term care centre for incapacitated persons on St. Jacques Street in lower downtown. Smiley had lost his second leg to gangrene. He was in a wheelchair which he could push by himself. He still had the big round Smiley smile, though he was alone most of the time. His memory had faded and the word "Houdini" seemed to have lost its meaning. He remembered my face and my beard, but couldn't recall much else.

"What did you say you do for a living?" he asked.

He wore a tweed cap and was munching on a sesame seed bagel, one of a half-dozen I brought him. Always the artist, pinned to the wall and piled on the dresser were sketches of each of the nurses on the floor,

December 1994. Sam Smiley at eighty-eight.
Photo by Don Bell

and of his visitors, including a helper named Neal who would take him outside when the weather was favourable. They liked to visit the antique stores on nearby Notre Dame Street. On the dresser were photos of his son and daughter and grandchildren, and two books—John Grisham's *The Firm* and Isaac Bashevis Singer's early short-story collection *Gimpel the Fool*. The last story he had read, Smiley said, was about Methusaleh. "Only thirteen pages but it was a marathon read."

Smiley in his wheelchair looked somewhat like a Methusaleh of Montreal, though he hadn't experienced family misfortunes anything like Singer's character Reb Moshe Ber. His son Charles visited as often as he could and his daughter Karen would come in from Maine during the summer. She had recently taken him out to the Red Lobster restaurant on the special bus which could accommodate his wheelchair, a treat because "lobster is his favourite food," as one of the nurses on Smiley's floor noted. "And he also," she added in a thick québécois accent, "loves schmaltzed herring." We went for a little ride around the floor, Smiley beaming in his wheelchair was obviously one of the staff's favourite residents. One of the nurses said that although legless and alone and pushing ninety, he was a man who didn't know the meaning of depression or melancholy.

Before leaving, I showed him two photos of his old McGill friend Jacques Price, one taken during the war in a Royal Canadian Air Force uniform, the other of Price as an old man.

"Do you recognize him?"

Smiley fondled the corner of the first picture, a matted eight-by-ten-inch black and white print, studied it for a while, then gazed at the second, a colour snapshot. I hadn't told him who the man in the pictures was. Smiley once said that he hadn't seen Price since they were students, which now would mean more than sixty years ago.

But there was still a flicker of memory.

"Is that Jacques?" Sam Smiley asked.

8

Pumpkinland

SAM SMILEY said he never saw Joscelyn Gordon Whitehead after the punching incident. The only news he had of him was from the lawyer Harry Cohen, who got Whitehead's affidavit early in 1927. Most of the literature on Houdini ends with words like those used in a Montreal *Gazette* article in 1986: "Criminal charges were never filed against Whitehead, and what became of him isn't known."

Starting in 1982, the search for Whitehead, or at least somebody who knew him and could describe what manner of man he was, became an obsession. Every Halloween I was out there sifting for clues.

Did he exist? Yes, it seemed so. McGill had a card for an Arts undergraduate in the 1926-27 school year named Joscelyn Gordon Whitehead. Joscelyn, usually spelled without the "s", is an old Scottish name, in earlier times often given to boys; it was introduced to Britain by Normans in the form of "Joscelin". This person was born in Gourock, Scotland, November 25, 1895, graduated from Kelowna High School, British Columbia, in 1914, and dropped out of McGill in 1926, almost immediately after the Houdini incident.

"His marks are such that they suggest he might have dropped out in any case," said a record-keeper in the Registrar's Office. There were no photos of him in *Old McGill*'s, and since he never graduated, the McGill Alumni Association had no address or any other information about him. Smiley had thought he was a divinity student, but a perusal of Faculty of Theology records draws a blank.

At one point I called Smiley to ask if he could have made a mistake on the name. The Faculty of Theology had a Gordon Campbell Wadsworth on its rolls in 1926. Wadsworth was from Nelson, B.C. and had worked on the *McGill Daily*. There was a Cecil Humphrey Whitemore, a member of the Student Christian Association. In 1927, there was Leslie Whitefield Blunden. Smiley said, no, he was sure Whitehead was the name.

Then why couldn't he be found in the comprehensive theology faculty records? Could Whitehead have said he was a divinity student to mock Houdini? Was Whitehead himself a believer in spiritualism, thus an arch-enemy of Houdini? Had he penetrated Houdini's dressing room to confront the non-believer, snidely telling him he was a divinity student, as one would say in a supercilious tone, "I'm a student of life."

If, as Smiley observed, he was an older student, in his late thirties when the incident took place in 1926, he would be in his eighties now. I wasn't hopeful of finding him alive, but surely there were people extant who knew him.

Calls for Mr. Whitehead or somebody who knew him were sent hither and yon in the early years of this probe, 1982 through 1986. If he was born in Scotland, perhaps "Her Majesty's Registration Office" in Edinburgh, as a Scottish friend suggested, could provide family background. But the Office wrote back saying that "the staff here do not undertake extensive searches which would be too time consuming." Her Majesty suggested arranging for someone to do the work, and furnished names of some Glasgow-based genealogists. Gourock, incidentally, is near Glasgow and, more exactly, is situated where Scotland's Firth of Clyde opens with a great bend to the south. Numerous ship collisions have taken place in these waters with great loss of life.

Could he be traced through Kelowna, British Columbia, where his family apparently settled after leaving Scotland? Perhaps he returned there after dropping out of McGill. I phoned Kelowna telephone directory assistance. They had two Whiteheads listed, a Frank and a Reg. Were they relatives? I tried Frank first, but the number was no longer in service. Then Reg. A pleasant-voiced fellow answered. No relation, he said right off, and he didn't know any other Whiteheads in the area except those in his immediate family. He was intrigued by the story, though—a namesake from Kelowna involved in this Houdini affair! He offered to phone back in a short while with some addresses that might be useful.

Half an hour later he rang while I was in the bath. "I didn't know easterners bathed," Reg Whitehead joked. He had found addresses and phone numbers for the Kelowna Museum Association which had an archives department, St. Michael and All Angels Anglican Church, which had parish records, and the Kelowna Detachment of the Royal Canadian Mounted Police.

I wrote to all three, to the RCMP explaining that "from all indications, Whitehead was an unsavoury character and perhaps had some criminal record. Although he'd be very old, it's possible that he might even still be alive, or at least there may be some descendants or relatives of Whitehead in the Kelowna area."

The RCMP superintendent replied quickly, citing "Our file/notre reference 84-28344" Regarding Joscelyn Gordon Whitehead: "This office failed to locate the above person you mentioned in your letter. Should you require further checks to locate the above or a relative of same, I would suggest you contact a private firm to carry out your request."

Not able to afford a private dick to find relatives of same, I carried on like Leacock's horseman "riding off in all directions."

The assistant curator of the Kelowna Museum Association, Dan Bruce, found a listing in the 1916 phone book for J.B. Whitehead, "which may have been his father," he wrote. It probably was, since Whitehead's McGill card gave his father's name as Joscelyn B. Whitehead. He promised to write again if the museum got any further with the search. The rector of St. Michael and All Angels Church, Rev. Canon J.A. Greenhalgh, replied also, saying that they had "searched all available parish and Diocesan records and have not been able to locate this man." And, curiously, since on his McGill card Whitehead was listed as graduating from Kelowna High School, Rev. Greenhalgh wrote that "Inquiries to the School Board Office have not turned up anyone by this name ever having been enrolled or graduating from Kelowna Secondary School."

Around this time, blurbs about the search were placed in Tommy Schnurmacher's social column in the Montreal *Gazette*, a call for Mr. Whitehead went out on CBC Radio, and letters to the editor were published in other Montreal and Toronto newspapers and the *McGill News* alumni magazine, calling for anyone who could provide information not only on Whitehead, but also on Smiley's friend Jacques Price, to please step forward.

No one did. It was like looking for two imaginary creations, characters who existed in a novel but had no tangible existence otherwise.

Since there were Whiteheads galore in Montreal and the heavily Anglo Eastern Townships of Quebec, any one of whom might have been related to J. Gordon, in 1984 I wrote a form letter describing the reasons for the search and sent it to each and every Whitehead listed in the Montreal and Townships phone directories. There were many replies, mostly from Whiteheads outlining their family histories, but saying unfortunately they didn't have any information about the Joscelyn or Gordon being sought. Some had stories to tell about the origin of the name.

J. Ralph Whitehead from Montreal's Town of Mount Royal suburb, for instance, said that when he was in the North of England a few years back, "I met some Whiteheads who claimed that the name came from an ancestor who was a highwayman. He was apprehended and lost his head to the sword. The head was placed on a pole, as a deterrent to other would-be highwaymen, and the hair turned white overnight. His family was referred to as the son, or daughter, of the white head! I can't tell how much truth there is in the story."

I half-expected the phone would ring in the middle of the night and there'd be a cadaverous voice on the line saying, "Hello. This is Gordon. I hear you've been looking for me." But there were no leads, not even an annoyed distant relative or acquaintance phoning to defend him or threatening a major lawsuit if I didn't let up.

My obsession went deep. My dreams offered revelations—or were they false leads? In one Bergmanesque dream sequence, a dentists' convention was being held at McGill and one of the dentists announced that Whitehead had been standing there in the conference room just a moment ago. I went straight to the registry desk and, sure enough, found a card on Joscelyn Gordon Whitehead with an address and a phone number, but unfortunately I woke up before being able to note them down. In the morning, I thumbed through the yellow pages, found a Montreal dentist named Whitehead and phoned him, certain he'd turn out to be Whitehead's relative, perhaps his son. Of course he wasn't, but this dream lead would be followed up in later research.

The legwork continued. I decided to pursue the stories in the Houdini literature that the author of the blow was a boxer or a football player. The *McGill Daily* didn't show Whitehead on any of the McGill boxing teams, nor did the Montreal newspapers list any Whiteheads on the pugilism cards at the Montreal Forum, circa 1926. And there was no one named Whitehead on any of the local gridiron clubs. Whitehead's name could not be found in any of the Montreal English-language dailies: the *Star*, *The Gazette*, *The Herald*, or *The Witness*.

The first break in tracing his name came in the fall of 1986. It was simple and obvious. I was at the McGill Archives in the basement of the Mac-Lennan Library, deep in research, checking Board of Governors minutes for December 20, 1926 and April 4 and June 20, 1927. There is no mention at all of Houdini lecturing at McGill or of any student punching him. Nor are there any clues in the thick three-volume *History of McGill University* by Stanley Frost. Robert Michel, a McGill archivist, had a thought. "Why not check the Mount Royal Cemetery where he might be buried if he was a Protestant?" he suggested. It is the biggest non-Catholic cemetery in the city.

I hastened to a public phone downstairs in front of the Redpath Library cafeteria, and called directory assistance for the number. A woman in the cemetery office, Edith Knowles, asked me to hold on for a moment while she checked the records. On the wall facing the row of telephones happened to be a garish poster advertising a McGill theatrical production of *Anatomy of a Murder*.

Mrs. Knowles returned to the phone.

"Yes," she said, "we do have Mr. Whitehead."

9

Death Notice

HE SEEMED to be our man. J. Gordon Whitehead—born in Scotland. Died July 5, 1954. The numbers matched. The Whitehead on the McGill records card who was born on November 25, 1895 would have been fifty-eight on July 5, 1954. Mrs. Knowles said he had been a patient at Queen Elizabeth Hospital in Montreal and apparently died of natural causes. A Dr. John McMartin signed the death certificate and Whitehead was brought in by a neighbour, Mabel Jackson. He was single, retired, and had no heirs. No religion was listed. He had a public burial at the government-owned Hawthorn Dale Cemetery, an annex of Mount Royal Cemetery, on Sherbrooke Street East near the oil refineries almost at the end of Montreal island. He could be found at Lot #188, Grave 75; there was no stone. The foreman would be in a green pickup truck and he could show you the plot, Mrs. Knowles explained.

Did she have an address for Whitehead? Yes, he had lived downtown at 1615 Lincoln, Apartment 11A.

After four years of pursuit, Whitehead had at last been found, reposing in an unmarked grave in a public Montreal cemetery. Now I could try to find people who knew him. Was Mabel Jackson still alive?

That evening I scanned the *Lovell's City Directories* on microfilm in the Gagnon Room of the Montreal Public Library. The directories have an alphabetical listing by name, and a listing by street name and occupant of dwelling. The 1954 as well as the 1955 *Lovell's* showed a Miss A.C. Matterson in Apt. 11A of the Grove Apartments at 1615 Lincoln. Could she have been Whitehead's girlfriend? The apartment appeared empty in 1953, but in 1952 a "Gordon W." was listed, probably Whitehead with his first name erroneously listed as his surname. However, in the alphabetical listing by name he was listed as Whitehead, Gordon, no profession.

The best bet for Mabel Jackson seemed to be a Miss M. Jackson listed in the 1954 directory in the Lincoln Row Apartments at 1618 Lincoln, Apt. 1, which would have been across the street from Whitehead. She was a secretary for Ross & Sons, Chartered Accountants.

Unfortunately, there was no way to look for old neighbours of Whitehead since the dwellings were long gone. There was a restaurant at what used to 1615 Lincoln near the corner of Guy, and a parking lot at 1618 where Miss M. Jackson lived.

But perhaps some of Whitehead's neighbours could nevertheless be found: for instance there had been a "Scales J.J., M.D." in Apt. 10. Was he still practising? Would one of the medical associations have an address for him?

Had there been a death notice for Whitehead in the Montreal newspapers? At the *Gazette* library the next day, sure enough, on July 7, 1954. "Whitehead. At the Queen Elizabeth Hospital on July 5, 1954, J. Gordon Whitehead. Funeral from D.A. Collins Chapel, 510 Sherbrooke Street West on Thursday, July 8, at 10 a.m." There was bizarre obituary on the same page, a story entitled "NAIL CAUSES DEATH", about a 17-year-old living in a trailer park in Hollywood, Florida, who yanked out his own abscessed tooth with a pair of pliers and probed for the root with a rusty nail, producing blood poisoning which killed him. Whitehead seemed to be close to dentists and dental problems, in my dreams and now in death. I checked the phone book for the funeral home on Sherbrooke Street West. It was at the same address, but was now called Collins, Clarke, MacGillivray and White. Without wasting a moment, I drove to the parlour, parked in front, and rang the bell.

10

An Answer from Limbo

As soon as Daniel Ryan learned the reason for my call was not to arrange a service but to inquire about a former "client", his expression changed from complicitous grief to curiosity. The Houdini story fascinated him, and he was most helpful.

He found a card for Whitehead. There wasn't much on it other than what the cemetery had, although it had a birth date, November 25, 1895, which corresponded to the McGill birth date, thus doubly confirming that the Whitehead buried at the Hawthorn Dale Cemetery was our man.

The card also had an address for Mabel Jackson: 1260 Mackay Street, just a block and a half away from the Lincoln Avenue apartment. I had gone through the Lovell's directories again and I knew that the M. Jackson living in the Lincoln Row Apartments across from Whitehead was not Mabel, but Muriel. The card showed that the Mabel Jackson on Mackay Street had given instructions for Whitehead's funeral bill to be sent to her in care of Mrs. Alex Reid on Logan Street in St. Lambert on Montreal's South Shore. Perhaps this Mrs. Reid could be traced and would know something.

Upstairs in the office Daniel checked through the funeral parlour's files for Mabel Jackson and Alex Reid in case they too had died and had had services there. There was a Mabel G. Jackson, who died in 1976. She lived on Grosvenor and was born in 1897. She had a brother at the same address and there was a phone number for him.

Later, I tried to call him, but the number had been disconnected. There were also a few deceased Reids, but no Alex. It seemed like a smarter idea to search amongst the living than the dead.

Could Dr. John McMartin, who wrote the death certificate, be found?

Queen Elizabeth Hospital, close to the funeral home, didn't have any doctors on staff by that name, but the College of Physicians and Surgeons had a listing for a Dr. John McMartin in Winnipeg.

"Sorry, wrong man. I never practised in Montreal," he told me over the telephone.

I wondered if the Queen Elizabeth had anything in their files on Whitehead. What was the cause of his death? I wrote to Dr. Eric Phelps, director of professional services. I knew that even if he did accept the reasons for the search, it would be next to impossible to find Whitehead's file because the hospital's present filing system was undertaken only in 1954 and files before that date, if they could be found at all, would be in old boxes in the hospital's archives.

Meanwhile, I was in touch with Magic Tom Auburn. Tom had always maintained that it was a McGill student boxer who had struck the blows at Houdini. What was his basis for thinking this, I asked over the phone.

Magic Tom recalled that some years ago he had been doing a show at a reception for Dr. Wilder Penfield at the McGill Faculty Club on McTavish. "There were a lot of medical people in the audience, and during the reception after, though I wasn't paying that much attention, I overheard a conversation about Houdini's death and one of the doctors who had been at McGill at the time said that it was a Dr. Whitehead who punched him after Houdini flexed his muscles, and he said this Whitehead fooled around with boxing at McGill."

Tom said he'd heard the story as well from the Montreal *Star* critic S. Morgan Powell. When he had been contacted by producers working on the movie *Houdini*, "They wanted to know if I knew the name of the chap who punched Houdini. I phone S. Morgan Powell because he had probably known Houdini personally from theatre circles, but he said, 'Why don't you let sleeping dogs lie?', so I just dropped it."

But sleeping dogs were being roused now. The day after dropping off my letter to Dr. Phelps at hospital, I phoned him. He said the cemetery may have had the doctor's name wrong since the hospital did have a Dr. *Jack* McMartin on its staff in 1954 who, in fact, had just left for Vancouver for two weeks, but it was his brother, the late Dr. Finley McMartin who was listed in the hospital registry as having treated Whitehead. But even if they did manage to track down the 1954 hospital record for Whitehead, it would probably just contain nurses' notes, Dr. Phelps explained. He confirmed that one hospital record showed that Whitehead had died of natural causes. He wasn't free to say what they were because of the hospital's policy of releasing medical information only to next-of-kin.

The Rare Book Room at McGill's MacLennan Library has paper copies of the *Lovell's City Directories*. I checked the directory for the name of the occupant at the Logan Street address in St. Lambert where Mrs. Alex Reid had lived in 1954. There was a Brian Moores now living at the address. His phone number was in the current phone book, and when I called him he was friendly and open and, like everyone else, intrigued by the Houdini story. He said he had bought the house from another owner, and he didn't know the Reids, but he understood that Mr. Reid was deceased, and Mrs. Reid might still be alive and living in senior citizens' home nearby. He would see if he could find the number and suggested calling back in a little while.

Back with the Lovell's in the Rare Book Room, I found some 1950s listings for the Mabel Jackson at 1260 Mackay Street. She had worked as a steno for Sun Life Insurance. I also searched for the Dr. John McMartin whose name was on the cemetery card. The closest was a J. McMartin who also worked for Sun Life. Was he a co-worker and friend who accompanied Mabel Jackson when she made the funeral arrangements? Had the cemetery mistakenly listed him as a doctor on Whitehead's death certificate?

I reached Brian Moore's again. He had found the number of the senior citizens' residence where Mrs. Reid was living. He also suggested contacting his neighbour Alf McKergow, who had been living on the street forty-five years or so and surely knew the late Alex Reid and Mrs. Reid. McKergow was a McGill graduate and a retired High School of Montreal teacher.

I called the old folks' home first. Mrs. Reid seemed confused. She was hard of hearing; I had to shout into the phone and repeat sentences to be understood. "Yes," she said, "I knew Mabel Jackson. She's living in

Vancouver." There was a long guarded silence when I mentioned White-head.

"How could one reach Mabel Jackson?" I asked.

She had changed her name, Mrs. Reid told me. Her new name was Versa Greene. Had she remarried? No, that wasn't the reason. She didn't elaborate. "You'll have to ask her yourself." Did she have phone number for her? Mrs. Reid gave me an address, Fremlin Street in Vancouver. The Vancouver area code was 604, she said, and the first three digits were 324. "You can phone Vancouver information," she said, as though not wanting to be held accountable for revealing the number.

"By the way, what is your relationship to Mabel Jackson?" I asked.
"What?"

"How did you happen to know her?"

"Of course I know her. She's my sister."

11

Vice Versa

⁓

BEFORE TRYING to reach Versa, I called Alf McKergow. Yes, he told me, he had been a McGill student and, yes, he had even been in the audience when Houdini lectured at McGill. He recalled Houdini explaining how he could wrestle himself free from any straitjacket restraint, and fulminating against the spiritualists, saying they were magicians like himself and he could duplicate any of their feats. But, alas, McKergow didn't know Whitehead and, at least at the lecture, wasn't aware of anyone punching Houdini, even by invitation.

He said he had been living at the St. Lambert address since 1945, and Mrs. Laurie Reid, who had lived a few doors away, was the late Alex Reid's second wife. His first wife had died in a fire in the 1940s. Laurie Reid was nicknamed "Jackie" because of her maiden name, Jackson. He couldn't recall ever having met her sister.

Later that day the hunt took on a new focus. I picked up some photocopied Houdini extracts that Magic Tom Auburn had left for me in a package at the news stand in the Dominion Square Building. Included were the final chapters of Milbourne Christopher's *Houdini: The Untold Story*. Reading through it in a nearby Hungarian restaurant, I came across a passage near the end declaring that fingerprints which Margery of Boston claimed were from her spirit guide Walter, and that had materialized in wax, were proved to be those of her dentist. Was this the tooth doctor? If there had been a plot to assassinate Houdini, could he have been one of the conspirators? Another avenue for future research.

I was joined at the table by an old friend, well-known downtown

Montreal personality Graham McKeen, a former concert pianist who
was heavily in the sauce but had corked the bottle on doctor's orders,
and now at fifty-four looked very fit. McKeen knew everybody; he had
consorted with Jack Kerouac and the Beats in the late 1950s, and was
friends with Norman Mailer, Leonard Cohen, and Robert Charlebois.

As we chatted, it suddenly struck me: could Graham have known
Whitehead? He would have been twenty-two in 1954 when Whitehead
died.

"Were you already downtown at that age?" I asked.

"Sure," Graham said in his raspy voice, as he sipped on a coffee.
"What did you say the fellow's name was, Gordie White?"

"No, Whitehead."

"Yeah, Gordie Whitehead. Sure. A tall fellow."

"You sure we're talking about the same person, Graham?"

"Sure I am. Gordie Whitehead."

"What do you remember about him?"

Graham tried to think back but his memory wasn't too clear. "Mario
Gross knew him well."

"Who's Mario Gross? Is he still alive?"

"Sure. He lives across the street from me. I'll speak to him. Phone
me tomorrow."

"How about Mabel Jackson?|"

"Yeah. Mabel Jackson. A singer."

"She used to work at Sun Life."

"That's her."

"You sure? She'd be around eighty now and she's living in Vancouver."

"That's her all right. Why don't you call me tomorrow. After six. I'll
speak to Mario."

"Could this be the big break?" I thought. After four years of pursuit,
finally an old bistro buddy tells you he knew Whitehead and would put
you in touch with others who had also known him. I decided I would
wait for news from Graham and complete my homework before phoning
Versa in Vancouver.

The next day, a lovely warm September Saturday afternoon, I dropped in on Laurie Reid at the Manoir St. Lambert. I hoped meeting her in person might bring better results than the call from the noisy McGill pay phone.

She was apprehensive at first, and the attendant who escorted me to her room and introduced us reassured her that it was all right. For a while we sat on the balcony, with its view of the St. Lawrence River. When it got chilly we moved onto cushioned armchairs in the lounge, where other seniors were reposing in chairs facing the window.

Mrs. Reid was eighty-three, frail, her face parched and sunken, her lips very taut. She had a trace of Scottish accent. I told her about the Houdini book and explained why I was interested in speaking to her sister.

My questions seemed a long way removed from this elderly woman's present reality. Yet she seemed to falter and throw up a wall when White-head's name came up, as though perhaps there was something she knew and couldn't say. She thought the best thing would be to call her sister in Vancouver. Mabel was eighty now, she said, and as far as she knew was in good health and most likely could speak to me.

"Do you want to speak to Mabel because of Whitehead?" she asked. I explained again the reasons for the research. "Whitehead was one of the last persons to see Houdini alive."

"You're doing all this only because you're writing a book?"

As I got up to leave, I mumbled something apologetic about it being my job; some people build bridges, others take up the pen.

"I'm sorry I haven't been able to help you much in that respect," she said. "I don't know very much about the subject."

In the evening I phoned Graham. He had spoken to his friend Mario Gross but apparently the Whitehead they knew wasn't Gordie but Harold, the portly late *Gazette* movie critic, well known in downtown circles. And Mabel Jackson was a Black nightclub singer. Another lead fizzled. As Yogi Berra once said, if you come to a fork in the road, take it. It was time to call Versa.

Vancouver directory assistance had the listing. It was Sunday evening.

Nervously, I dialled the number, feeling Houdini must be standing invisible over my shoulder, waiting for results.

Someone picked up the phone, but didn't speak.

"Hello. May I speak to Versa Greene?" I asked.

"Who is this?" replied a man with a squishy voice.

12

Favery

Briefly, I told him that I was doing some research for a magazine article and eventually a biography on Harry Houdini. I recapitulated the incident in the dressing room, mentioning that there were three students present when Houdini received the fatal punch and one was Joscelyn Whitehead. I took care not to finger him as the one who did the actual punching. I told him I had been in touch with a Mrs. Laurie Reid in Montreal who said that her sister Mabel Jackson, at that number, had known Whitehead. I wondered if I could speak with her.

"The only thing I can suggest is that you write to us. What did you say your name was?"

I told him.

"And who am I speaking to, by the way?" I added.

"Favery O'Connor."

"Are you Mrs. Jackson's husband or relative?"

"Let's say I'm a relative. When did you speak to Mrs. Greene regarding this?"

"I haven't. I've only spoken to her sister, Mrs. Reid, who told me she was living in Vancouver. I've been trying to trace her for quite some time. It's my understanding that she knew Whitehead," I insisted.

"What was his first name?"

"Joscelyn." I spelled it out for him. He didn't recognize the name. "Gordon? Joscelyn Gordon Whitehead?"

"Oh, oh, oh, okay."

"It all goes back a long time. Apparently your relative knew him rather well. Has she ever spoken to you about him?"

"Houdini's last act," he asked, "was when?"

"His last act? In 1926. This Halloween will mark the sixtieth anniversary of his death. Whitehead knew him in 1926."

"Who knew him?"

"Whitehead. And Mrs. Greene knew Whitehead, which is the reason I'm phoning her. I'm trying to find out as much as I can on Whitehead. Who he was. What sort of a man. Did he have any next-of-kin, any relatives in Montreal, how he was affected by the death of Houdini. Standard journalistic questions. Because of this, uh, historical biography on Houdini, my investigations have led me to Mrs. Greene, to yourself, to this phone number. So I was wondering if I could speak to Mrs. Greene. Is she there now?"

"Well, let me have your address, will you please, Mr. Bell?"

"I will. The thing is, is she in good health?"

"Yes, she is in good health."

"Is she with you now?"

"Yes."

"Well, I would like to have a word with her. Can she come to the phone now?"

"Well, she has a hearing problem."

"Is she totally deaf?" I asked.

"She hears, as long as she has good batteries."

"How did you say you are related to her? Or are you just a friend?"

"We're related. But I'm quite distant."

"Are you living with her now?"

"I live in Seattle. I happen to be up here visiting."

"What would be the best way to proceed?" I asked.

"You should write down the questions that you would like to have answered, that are pertinent to your investigation, and we will correspond with you."

"Perhaps I can just tell you what some of the questions are now on the phone," I suggested. "Would you be able to communicate them to Mrs. Greene?"

"I can try."

"For instance, does she know anybody else who might still be alive who—"

"Sixty years after the fact? I doubt it."

"Well, it's not sixty years," I explained. "We're talking about 1954, when Whitehead died."

"You wouldn't happen to know the date on that?"

"July 5. Mrs. Greene had arranged the funeral and burial. What I'd be interested in finding out from her is if she knows if Whitehead had any relatives or next-of-kin. And also, did he ever talk to her about the Houdini incident?"

"I don't know. He was very sick."

"Did you know Whitehead yourself?"

"No, I didn't. I never had that opportunity."

"How did Mabel know him?"

"Her name is no longer Mabel," he corrected.

"Did she change it for any particular reason?"

"Yes. The vibrations in her name were terrible."

"Vibrations? You mean because of her hearing problem?"

"No, just the vibrations. Do you have a middle name, Mr. Bell?"

"Yes."

"What is it?"

"Uh … Herbert."

"You're a very quiet person, aren't you?"

"You mean the sound of the name, the vibrations are—"

"The universe is made up of vibrations. Your thoughts are vibrations. When your heart pumps blood through your body, that's a vibration. Your name and birth date is a vibration. She asked me to change the name so she could have one with a more pleasant vibration."

"Are you a psychic person yourself?" Today's numerologist could be yesterday's irate medium. If Whitehead had consorted with members of such a, well, cult, he may have seen Houdini as an enemy.

"I'm not psychic but intuitive," Favery O'Connor answered.

"What do you do for a living, Mr. O'Connor?"

"Well, I do many things, between driving a cab, herbalism, healing, music, poetry, singing, and of course I give readings."

"What about Mrs. Greene? Does she have similar interests?"

"She used to be an organ player. She lectured and travelled a lot.

She's also into numerology. But she's more or less, well, kind of slowed down a bit, if you know what I'm saying. She's eighty now. She doesn't lecture as much as she used to, or travel or teach as much."

"Where did she play the organ?"

"Well, she played it out in Montreal."

"Was Joscelyn a musician as well?"

"I'll find out. Hold on. It's on your time."

Favery had a few words with Versa then returned to the phone.

"He has a brother out here in Vancouver."

"Do you have a phone number and an address for him?" I asked.

"Sure. It must be costing you a pretty penny. What paper did you say you were with?"

"When you're not around," I asked, while he was looking for the brother's number in the Vancouver directory, "is there anybody else, if I phoned Mrs. Greene again and had something specific to ask, who would be able to communicate with her?"

"Well, if you want to talk to her now, hold on. Versa," he called, "would it upset you to talk to the man about—" There was a muffled voice in the background. "She doesn't want to talk. She's too upset."

"Why would she be upset?"

"She's just upset. Okay, the brother is—." He gave an address and phone number.

"Does she know if Gordon had any other relatives or friends? Perhaps people still around in Montreal who might have known him?"

"I don't think so. But I'll talk to her later about it. She's a little upset. It's quite unexpected."

Favery passed on his own address in Seattle, "just in case our wires get crossed somehow."

"Do you have a phone?"

"Well, I'm not ever there. And when I'm there, I'm not there for phone calls. When I'm home, I don't particularly like to have calls."

"Do you know what kind of work Whitehead did?" I asked, one last cast, still fishing for clues.

"I couldn't say because like I told you I very seldom discussed him with her. Well, we'll certainly do as much as we can to help you in your research," Favery O'Connor said. "Just one more question. What is your date of birth?"

I told him.

"A good year. Yes, a very good year."

"I may come to Vancouver. I'd like to meet Mrs. Greene, and your-self."

"Well, I'll talk to Mrs. Greene about it, but I think it would be a good idea if you wrote down your questions first, with a breakdown on paper of what you'd like to know, and we'll write to you as soon as possible."

"Can you reply by special delivery?"

"Yes, we can do that, Mr. Bell," said Favery O'Connor, as we concluded our conversation.

I sent a package addressed to Versa Greene "or Favery O'Connor". I included, besides a letter, an empty ninety-minute audio cassette tape, a self-addressed jiffy bag, and a five-dollar bill to cover return postage. I suggested in a note to Favery that it might be easier for Versa "to talk into a tape recorder with her recollections about Gordon Whitehead than to write." The letter contained a list of questions for Mrs. Greene.

Did he have emotional or psychological scars because of the incident? Did he have any remorse? Did he talk to you about it or was it a "skeleton-in-the-closet" situation, a part of his past which he preferred buried? Particularly, would you have any photos of Joscelyn, or did he leave any diaries or letters, or documents of any kind that would reveal more about him and the Houdini incident?

There has been a lot of speculation, Mrs. Greene, about the Princess Theatre incident. [I once again gave a synopsis of the incident, mentioning the theories that Whitehead's blows may have been more than just an innocent student prank.] Anything that you know would certainly shed valuable light on the subject, even though it took place so long ago. Did Joscelyn, for instance, mention to you what book it was that he had been returning to Houdini, or how he happened to know Houdini? I realize this may be a very sensitive issue for you, but it would be most interesting to know the full story behind the episode.

If Houdini was deliberately, not haphazardly, punched by Joscelyn, well, why must it be necessary to defend him now? But if this was not the case, then an effort should be made to clear Whitehead's name from any suspicion of wrongdoing. Since you knew Joscelyn so well, and are well-acquainted with the facts, you may be the only person who can help solve the puzzle surrounding Houdini's death and reveal the whole story. Most Houdini historians think there is more to the incident than has been made public, if only because Joscelyn seemed to vanish into thin air after the punching sequence, and was never heard from again. In fact, until finding his death certificate at the cemetery, and then making other verifications, I wasn't even sure myself that Joscelyn Gordon Whitehead had truly existed.

13

A Brother Found

THE PHONE CALL at least confirmed that J. Gordon Whitehead had existed. And it established that he had some bizarre cronies. Was it unreasonable to assume that in 1926 Whitehead may have been consorting with odd characters? Did he know any of the mediums operating out of Montreal? Was he a closet spiritualist?

It remained to be seen if Versa Greene's friend was the same Whitehead who had been in Houdini's dressing room. The man in the cemetery file and whose card was in the funeral home still hadn't been conclusively linked to Houdini.

Next day I called Whitehead's brother. (To protect the family's privacy, I won't give the first name and profession.) His wife answered. After I told her it was long distance from Quebec, but not explaining the reason for the call, she asked her husband to come to the phone.

"Hello, Mr. Whitehead, how are you?"

"Not bad."

"What's the weather like in Vancouver now?"

"Vancouver. It's way ahead of itself. It's very good."

"I hear it's always raining. But you've had a good summer there this year with the Fair?" In 1986 Vancouver was hosting the World's Fair and the city was in a euphoric mood.

"Oh, hell, yes. We haven't had any rain for well over a month. Forty-odd days."

"Mr. Whitehead, the reason I'm phoning you is …"

I explained without going into too much detail. The brother was eighty-two at the time of the call. It is no doubt disconcerting to suddenly find oneself at such a ripe age being grilled, politely, but grilled all the same, about a far-back fishy smelling incident. There was a stunned non-response, but eventually Mr. Whitehead saw fit to reminisce, albeit protectively, about his younger brother Gordon.

"It's probably a sensitive issue for you, for your family, but I was wondering," I began, "if you'd be willing to talk to me about it. If you could tell me anything about Joscelyn, how it affected his life, if he—"

"Well, I don't understand," he broke in. He had a stammering James Stewart kind of wattle-larynxed voice. "Why should you be writing on Houdini? He's been written about a great deal already, hasn't he?"

"Of course, but—"

"What is it that especially attracts you to writing about him, now?"

"Well, I guess because I'm a Montrealer, originally, and since the incident took place in Montreal—"

"What incident do you refer to?"

"Well, it's been written about in some of the biographies. There were three students who went into his dressing room. Houdini used to boast that he could withstand any punch to his stomach, and apparently one of the three students, uh, tested him, and Houdini, well, according to the legend—of course nobody is sure whether this is true or not, which is what I'm trying to find out—Houdini didn't have to time to get himself properly, flexed, for the punch, and there was an injury, and he, uh, died nine days later in Detroit, on Halloween."

"Why didn't he give himself the time to prepare for this punch, if he was maintaining that he could withstand any punch that he received?"

"I don't know. But one of the students happens to be still alive, and he says Houdini was reclined on the couch, going through his mail, and Joscelyn came into the room. He apparently knew Houdini and was returning a book which he had borrowed. They talked for a while about religion, or spiritualism, and of course Houdini had been exposing the fraudulent mediums at the time, and then—this has all been written about, it's in several of the books about Houdini—Joscelyn asked if he could, uh, try, uh, you know, punch Houdini, and I guess Houdini nodded, said yes, but—"

"Who, who asked that?"

"Well, Joscelyn did."

"Joscelyn?"

"Yes."

"Joscelyn? I don't get it. Did Joscelyn—?"

"Aren't you the brother of Joscelyn Gordon Whitehead?"

"Ohhh, ohhh. Yes, yes, I had a brother by that name. Yes. But he was never known as 'Joscelyn.'"

"Gordon?"

"Yes. All right. Now you're saying he was a friend of Houdini's. He came into the room, when Houdini was reclining on a couch. And he was returning a book that he had borrowed from Houdini. And he entered into some sort of conversation with Houdini."

"And then," I continued, "he apparently asked Houdini if he could test him, with this, uh, blow to the stomach. I wasn't in the dressing room, of course, but according to the popular version, Houdini really didn't bother to prepare himself, and Gordon, well, if he was your brother, hit him once or twice, and Houdini said it was okay, but the other students were worried about Houdini getting hurt. They jumped up and they, uh, pulled Gordon away from him. Did Gordon ever talk to you about this incident?"

"No."

"He never did?"

"He was very much a loner."

"Was he ever married, or did he have any children?"

"No."

"What kind of work did he do?" I asked.

"I really don't know too much. The last employment that I know that he had, he was a Montreal correspondent for the *New York Times*."

"Was he on staff?"

"I know very, very little about him."

"How close were you in age?"

"He was my older brother. He was eight years older. He was the oldest member of the family, and I'm the youngest."

"Are there other brothers and sisters in between?" I inquired.

"There are, yes, but—there were, I should say. I have a sister who is still alive."

"Did she know Gordon very well?"

"No."

"Is she living in Vancouver?"

"Well, I don't know that I'm prepared to give you her address. You're simply a voice over the telephone and you're giving me information, and I can only take it on face value and so on and so forth. I don't know what it is that you are searching for, and why you should be phoning me. I mean, this incident, it happened very, very many long years ago. And you say your publishers asked you to dig into the life of Houdini? It has been well researched already, hasn't it?"

"Well, yes, but little is known about the end of Houdini's life, and because it's a Montreal story as I said, and being a Montreal writer, it particularly fascinates me. This Halloween will be the sixtieth anniversary of Houdini's death, so I though I'd try to write a story about, uh, Houdini's performance in Montreal. And since so little is known about the incident in the dressing room, being curious, I thought—"

"Are you an independent journalist?"

"A freelance writer for major Canadian magazines. I've had a couple of books published."

"What are your books?"

"Well, the first one was *Saturday Night at the Bagel Factory*, sort of a collection of stories about Montreal, set in the 1960s."

"What's the title of it?"

"*Saturday Night—*"

"*Saturday Night?*"

"Yes, *at the Factory*."

"The *Factory?*"

"Yes."

"Those were the two books you wrote?"

"No. The other one is called *Pocketman*."

"*Talking Man?*"

"No. *Pocket*, like the pockets on your pants?"

"All right. Okay. We got that. Now, you're phoning me as a relative of J. Gordon Whitehead?"

"Right."

"Who was involved in an incident with Houdini, and you want to know whether I know anything about that?"

"About that and also about your brother, who he was, and if he ever talked to you about the incident."

"My brother was not given to talking with me, or to people, about his own private life. He was a fine man, he did very wonderful things for me. I certainly was never close to him, and he was not a man that one could get close to, but he was remarkable in the people he got to know. For instance, how in the wide world did he ever get to know Houdini and get to have the, apparently personal relationship that he had with him? I know of many other outstanding people that he had close relationships with, but how he got to know them, I couldn't say."

"You said he knew other famous people?"

"Oh, yes. He knew a great number of prominent people in industry, in education."

"Did your brother spend most of his life in Montreal?"

"Well, he spent a good part of his life there. He was in and out of Montreal. I had no idea where he was most of the time, and got no information as to what he'd been doing. That's the way he was. I was a younger brother, he was the older brother and I respected him, and as I say, I'm very greatly indebted for having him as an older brother. But I really didn't know very much about him. When I first went to Montreal, he was there. He was a purser with CPR, on the boats, travelling between Montreal and the Great Lakes. But the vast majority of the time I don't know how he earned his income. I'm sure he wasn't into illicit endeavours of any kind. He was not that kind of man. But what he did do or where and how he earned his money, I really don't know."

"Do you know if he had any special interests?"

"Oh, yes. He had so many interests. He was a very intense person. I never saw him read a newspaper without a dictionary on one side and an atlas on the other. He wanted to know about things, and made it his business to find out about them and he didn't fool around. He went straight to the horse's head."

"Is there anybody that he was very close to in Montreal, that might still be alive, who knew him?"

"I know that at one time he had a close relationship with a wealthy, well, round about his own age, woman. Who she was, what she was exactly, I don't know. He had a very close association with her. He never got married. I don't think he ever actually got engaged to anyone."

"Is that Mabel Jackson that you are referring to?"

"Eh?"

"Would her name be Mabel Jackson?"

"I have no idea what her name was. As I say, I know nothing about— Who's Mabel Jackson?"

"Well, apparently she's the person who arranged the funeral service when he died in 1954."

"Well, if you've got any information about that, I'd— I would appreciate having it because I got nothing. It just happened. I don't know how I got to hearing about his death, but it happened that a friend of mine who was a lawyer in Ottawa was in Montreal, and I asked him to deal with whatever was necessary. But all I learned from him … he gave me really no information. I never saw an obituary notice. I don't know whether this Mabel Jackson has one. If she had, I certainly would be delighted to have it."

"There was a short notice in the *Gazette* at the time, just for one day and not very much information in it."

"I'd be interested to know what the hell it was."

"I have a photocopy of it and can send it to you," I offered.

"I'd appreciate that and as I say, I think that was where, through this lawyer friend of mine, that I got the information that he was a correspondent with the *New York Times*."

[I later checked this lead with the *New York Times*, which has a byline index. But Whitehead's name didn't show; nor could any entries be found under his name in Canadian periodical indexes.]

"Do you know if he was ever a boxer?" I asked.

"Oh, no. No."

"In some of the versions, it's said that it was a boxer who hit, that had gone into Houdini's dressing room and—"

"I certainly didn't know that he was a boxer. He was an extremely powerful man, in many ways. He was long, and lean. I know that when he was attending McGill University, and he had to blow … I don't know, some chest testing. And they had a machine there, and he blew the thing right out. So he went back the next day, and they had another machine there. He did the same thing again, blew it right out! I don't know how he developed that, but as I say, there's so much I don't know anything about, but I couldn't see him as being avidly involved in boxing, certainly not professional. But I knew a hell of a lot better than to fool around with him, not that we had that kind of relationship, mind you, but I can appreciate that if he undertook to deliver a blow to somebody they would certainly know who it was, that it wasn't some kid."

"He was quite tall?"

"We're all fairly tall men. I'm just under six-foot one, and I think he was over six-one, close to six-two. I don't know what his weight would be, but judging by my own, as a six-foot one man, my weight never varied much between 165 and 167 pounds, and he was the same type. He certainly wasn't a 200-pound man."

"Would you have any photos of him?" I asked.

"Yes, I have one."

"There's a chance," I said, "that I'll be in Vancouver, some time in the next month, and possibly, I was wondering if I could take a look at it? Maybe make a copy of the photograph, would that be possible?"

"Well, it might be. I can think about it between now and the time that you will arrive. And you know, this Margery Nichols you say, that took charge of the—"

"No, Mabel Jackson."

"Mabel Jackson. Well, if you know how she came to get into the picture, if you find out anything about that…"

"I will. You mentioned the name Margery Nichols. Is that the friend of Gordon's?"

"That's because I'm not as young as I used to be. Mabel Jackson and Margery Nichols, I confused—"

"You sound in great shape for eight-two."

"So my doctor tells me. I try to take that as a responsibility of age, keep as well as possible."

Whitehead now talked about his own background and professional life. He said he had been in Montreal during World War II, because of his older brother being there, and stayed for about twelve years. At one time he lived for a couple of months with Gordon.

"But I didn't see him often. Sometimes we'd go for three or four months, and I'd never hear from him."

"Was Gordon," I asked, "involved in, or was he at all interested in, esoteric things, like spiritualism, or astrology, things like that?"

"Well, I'm sure he had an interest in them, yes, and I'm sure that probably that was one of the things that drew him to Houdini, or how he was able to establish a relationship with Houdini. He probably discussed that sort of thing with Houdini. It's well known of course that Houdini did say that there was no medium that he couldn't expose. Didn't he have a standing offer of a thousand dollars or something of the kind? So as I say, I am not able to give you any information like that because I just don't know it."

"Are you sure that Gordon never really talked about Houdini that much? It would seem to me that it might have affected his life if he—"

"Oh, no. He never talked to me at all. He merely said that, I think, he knew Houdini, and I think he may have said that he visited him once in his dressing room or something like that, but that would be all that I would know about any relationship."

"Do you think he knew Houdini before Houdini performed in Montreal?"

"What?"

"That he might have met him previously? Maybe in another city, like New York, or Boston, or Philadelphia?"

"I have no idea. Gordon could have been in any of those places, but I wouldn't have known anything about it, because, as I say, there were long periods of time when we didn't have any contact. There was no detailing of what had gone on in the meantime. He was an unusual man. I don't think of him at all as an eccentric, but unusual, certainly. I know of no one like him, and I'm indebted to him in many ways. He taught me so much about living. He was a well-dressed person. He taught me how to look respectable in the clothes that I wore. How to handle a knife and fork. Don't forget, we moved from a very simple home life in British

Columbia to a life in Montreal, which was much more sophisticated. But that's about all I can tell you about him. As I say, he was a very private person, nobody really knew him."

I sent Mr. Whitehead a letter, including a copy of the obituary notice and a (not entirely accurate) description of the dressing-room incident photocopied from the Amazing Randi and Bert Sugar book, which does at least identify Gordon Whitehead as the author of the blow or blows. I asked him again if he was aware of any letters or other documents about the Houdini affair. I also asked if he could remember any friends his brother had in or around Montreal or what circles he was in, and whether he could recall anything further about the "well-to-do woman" Gordon had been consorting with in Montreal.

14

No Clues Are Good Clues

Vancouver seemed likely to hold the key. But before making any bookings, it seemed sensible to try to find out more about Mabel. What was Whitehead's relation to her? Was she his girlfriend at the end of his life? Could she have dabbled in spiritualism or mediumship?

When Mabel worked at Sun Life, the twenty-two storey building was the tallest in Montreal, a city landmark. From the lookout on top of Mount Royal, it was the most impressive building in the skyline, a granite temple that seemed almost as wide as it was tall. I recall as a youngster the euphoria of clopping through the marble-floored lobby and taking the elevator to the sixth floor where the National Hockey League and *Hockey News* offices were located. Schedules and photos of hockey stars were available for the asking. The building also housed the Belgian and Peruvian consulates and the tourist boards of Barbados, British Guiana, Grenada, and Jamaica, whose representatives were usually delighted to tear off cancelled postage stamps on envelopes and give them to excitable young philatelists (my friends and me) making the consular rounds on Saturday mornings once every month or so.

The insurance company then had 3,000 employees and occupied the first few floors, which it still does, although the building is now dwarfed by others across the Montreal the skyline.

I called Sun Life's personnel department.

She was found under her new name, Versa Greene, at the present Vancouver address. She had worked in the Policy Loans office in the 1950s. Most of her old bosses had died, but it was propitious timing because the next day there would be a meeting of the company's Drop-In Pensioners' Club in the seventh-floor staff lounge.

The pensioners, mostly women sixty and over, sat around a conference table. Minutes were read, then there was a "By the way, we have a guest here today who would like to talk to you about his project on Harry Houdini."

I briefly described it. Whitehead wasn't known to any of the members. As far as Mabel was concerned, some of them recalled meeting her at a Vancouver reunion a few years ago.

But one of her ex-colleagues (who asked not to be named) came over during tea and biscuits and said she remembered Mabel as "old-fashioned type of person, a little bit old-maidish. She was short and slight with a very erect back. She didn't slump. She used to do eye exercises because she needed glasses, and I remember that she had a small lump, about the size of a pea, on the tip of her tongue. And she was, well, eccentric, a bit of an odd person. She took an interest in a much wider variety of things than we do now." What kind of things? Spiritualism? The former colleague couldn't say. Just "a wide variety".

Could this wide variety have included musical endeavours? As Favery had revealed, Mabel was an organist and had performed somewhere in Montreal. Was she known in musical circles? Was Whitehead?

I phoned the Christ Church Cathedral downtown, known for its organ concerts, and asked Father Derby, the vicar, if he knew either Mabel Jackson or Gordon Whitehead. No, but he'd been at the church only five years, he said. He'd ask some of the older parishioners and if he had any luck he would get back. He suggested trying Kenneth Meek, an organist who had been around a long time. I did, but Meek didn't know them either.

But perhaps Mabel's passion—or Whitehead's—had been popular music. Wally Aspell, a downtown entertainer "for donkey's years" who knew everyone in the city, couldn't recall Mabel Jackson. Aspell said a lot of businessmen frequented the club where he played and he'd ask around. "Come into the club for a drink sometime," he offered.

No clues were good clues.

If Whitehead was an avid reader, as his brother mentioned, he might be remembered by some old librarians. The most logical place to search was the Atwater Library near the Montreal Forum, not far from the Lincoln Street apartment. It has a large selection of books on the occult and supernatural, if such was his field of interest. A lady at the reference desk provided names of various octogenarian and nonagenarian librarians who might be alive but more likely were dead. I found two who were still on this plane, but, alas, they couldn't recall any library borrower who signed his card J. Gordon Whitehead and who took out books on spiritualism and Harry Houdini.

I had not forgotten the CP purser lead. "Hi, Don Bell," chanted the answering machine. "It's Mike Spinnard from CP Rail in Montreal. I haven't been able to come up with anything at all either from our archives or from our pension records. This guy probably didn't even collect a pension if he was only with us for a few years, so from our end it seems like a dead end. But the people who were looking into it will keep on as much as they can. If I come up with anything, I'll let you know. You have my number if you want to call back. Take care."

In itself, this didn't seem particularly important, one more clue that fizzled out. It seemed that everything I discovered about Whitehead was turning out to be a mirage. He was a divinity student who wasn't a divinity student, a boxer who wasn't a boxer. He was *New York Times* correspondent who apparently never worked for the *Times*. He was a purser on Canadian Pacific ships, but CP had no employment record of him. He lived in Montreal, but wasn't known to anyone in Montreal. He was in Houdini's dressing room to return a book, but nobody could say what book or if he knew Houdini.

I phoned the Mount Royal Cemetery and asked when the gates to the Hawthorn Dale east-end annex would be open. It might be as close as anyone would ever get to J. Gordon Whitehead.

15

The Cemetery

IT WAS A SPLENDID AUTUMN afternoon when I went calling on White-head. The trees were ablaze with scarlet and cinnamon leaves. The municipal cemetery out on Sherbrooke Street East was a complete contrast to downtown which was teeming with traffic and shoppers; here, everything was quiet and, well, perfectly dead.

I found the foreman in the green pickup truck which Mrs. Knowles at the office said to look for. He pointed to a gravedigger up the road and said he would know exactly where Lot #188, Grave #75 was located.

The gravedigger, a wizened, scraggly man in his fifties, said "Suis-moi" and tramped to a patch of trimmed outfield grass on which fallen leaves were scattered. He checked a few markers, then stopped on a bare spot between two flat stones embedded in the ground which were marked Alexander Dudidenko and Otto Lottemoser.

"C'est iz'itte qu'i repose," he said, standing on Whitehead's plot and leaning on his shovel. He stayed there for a moment, his face registering sympathy for the dear departed and the mourner paying his respects. "C'est toujours tranquille iz'itte," he remarked, then picked up his shovel and left me there alone, six feet from the object of my search.

It was absolutely still, the afternoon sun casting tall shadows on the grass. I had a camera and took a few photos of my magnified shadow on top of Whitehead's grave. Because of its length and oblong form, the flattened-out shadow looked like a scene-of-the-crime police photo, a telltale image perhaps of the tall mysterious visitor to Houdini's dressing room whose remains reposed beneath.

A woman with a dog was approaching along the cemetery road. She saw I was taking photos of shadows on the ground, and, curious, stopped

J. Gordon Whitehead's final resting place—Mount Royal
Cemetery, Montreal, Quebec
Photo by Don Bell

to watch. I left the grave site and walked toward her. She was stunningly beautiful, with glistening mahogany eyes. The dog which was off hopping among the tombstones was a strain of Labrador. We talked for a while. She was a radiologist, half Italian, had just returned from a posting in Saudi Arabia; she lived nearby and enjoyed walking her dog in the cemetery because it was so peaceful, like another world, she said. She asked if I was visiting a grave. I told her briefly about Houdini and Whitehead. "Can you show me where he is?" she asked in French. Her coat was chestnut-coloured and fastened to her waist with a thin belt, the ends of which dangled down like pompoms and bounced against her thighs as she moved. Her hair fell in long swirls behind her shoulders and down her back.

We strolled to the plot; my head was spinning. It was ridiculously Bunuelian: death and desire. It's here, I told her. We were now standing inches apart on top of the bones of Whitehead. She wore a touch of perfume. I could feel its mist on my cheeks. Is he under us? she asked. The gravedigger had gone off and there were only the stones, the shadows, and us.

Standing on Whitehead's grave, I felt something rising up inside myself. A magician's wand? Was it the puissant spirit of Houdini being awakened? Just then the green pickup truck drove up the road and stopped, and the foreman got out. He thought the radiologist was my companion and asked if we had found the plot.

Then he explained why persons were buried here rather than up on the mountain; he described the cemetery's growth, its future growth, other interesting gardens in the city, the benefits of a hand-dug grave as opposed to a bulldozed hole-in-the-ground, staff problems at Mount Royal Cemetery, and the pros and cons of the gravediggers' union.

She had walked off with her chien.

She was like a phantom in the dusk. Dante's radioactive Beatrice, or Houdini's? I couldn't find her and never saw her again.

16

The Mysterious Lodger

∾

STILL ON THE PROWL, I wondered what I could find out about Whitehead from his neighbours. It would take some sleuthing but surely one or two could be found who would remember the tall fellow in 11A. There was, for instance, the "Scales J J M.D." listed in the Lovell's for 1952, the same year "Gordon W" lived in the Grove Apartments. He had been in Apt. 10, which must have been on the same floor as Whitehead. He wasn't listed in the current Montreal phone book, but perhaps could be traced through medical associations.

The librarian at the McGill Medical Library's reference desk found a Dr. Joseph J. Scales listed in the Canadian Medical Directory. He was a general anaesthetist practising at Edmonton General Hospital. No doubt our man.

I phoned him immediately. Friendly, and fascinated by the story, he confirmed that he and his wife Theresa had lived in the Grove Apartments on Lincoln in 1952. He had been doing post-graduate work at McGill then and had left Montreal for Edmonton the same year. They didn't mix much with the neighbours, Dr. Scales said, because he and his wife were both extremely busy with their studies. It was going back thirty-odd years. Still, he remembered the building and the life around it—the landlady, an old man with one leg who lived upstairs. The name White-head didn't ring a bell, but he recalled that there had been a mysterious lodger in 11A across the hall. "He was gone all day and returned in the middle of the night, usually after midnight. We never conversed with him, though."

On a couple of occasions he passed in front of the apartment when the door had been left open.

"The reason I remember it is because the apartment was stacked from floor to ceiling with piles of old newspapers. To get in, there was a little pathway through the newspapers. That's the only way you'd be able to enter.

"It was a three-storey brick building with very thick walls—adequate, but old," he recalled. "We had two bedrooms with a kitchen and living room. I believe all the other dozen or so apartments, including 11A, were designed the same way. I remember that there was a fire at the Montreal Repertory Theatre across the lane. It completely burned down. We had a fair amount of water damage. There was a lot of excitement and it was an occasion to meet most of our neighbours, including a couple with two children who lived on the top floor. But we didn't meet Whitehead, if he was the recluse in 11A."

After he and his wife moved to Edmonton, two nurses his wife knew who were employed at the Royal Victoria Hospital took over the apartment. They would have been there from 1952 to 1954 when Whitehead died. By chance, the nurses also ended up in Edmonton. It would be no trouble to find their phone numbers, Dr. Scales said. "They might remember more than we do." He had been conferring with his wife throughout the conversation. "Also there was another anaesthetist on the same floor as us, Dr. Rudolph Ohkle. He ended up practising somewhere in Ontario. He might have known Whitehead. I wish I could remember more, but the old brains don't go back that far."

As it turned out, the nurses, now Mrs. Doris Hoe and Mrs. Lola Ross, couldn't recall much more than Dr. Scales, although they did confirm that living in 11A there had been "an eccentric who came in at odd hours."

Meanwhile, the Ontario College of Physicians and Surgeons found Dr. Rudolph Frank Ohkle in its listings. He had practised in Mississauga, but he was now deceased. For the moment it seemed unlikely that any other neighbours would be found who knew Whitehead.

It was mid-October 1986. The World's Fair was still on in Vancouver. I needed a holiday. There were also two kindly uncles in Vancouver who hadn't been seen in a long time. And, well, I might just drop in on Versa Greene and Favery O'Connor, and Kelowna was not all that far from Vancouver.

17

Marjorie of Montreal

WHITEHEAD'S BROTHER never answered my letter, but there was a prompt reply from Favery O'Connor. My jiffy bag and empty cassette were returned, and there was a crumpled note scribbled on a page of lined foolscap at the bottom of the package.

> Dear Sir,
> We regret that we can be of no help in this matter. Miss Greene never knew anything of Gordon's personal life. However, if you can, trace a Marjorie Goldstein, former language teacher who coached the boys at McGill and who lived on Ste. Catherine Street West, Westmount, and who had known Gordon's personal life very well.
> > Sincerely,
> > Favery O'Connor for Versa Greene

Was Marjorie of Montreal the wealthy woman whom Whitehead's brother said Gordon had been seeing? He said her name was Margery, or Marjorie, Nichols. Was it a slip of the tongue?

The ever-reliable McGill Archives office had something on her, but the news was not good. A death notice appeared in the *McGill News* alumni magazine in April 1966. "Miss H. Marjorie Goldstein, BA '14, MA '16, at Montreal on October 18, 1965." The "Miss" meant it was unlikely she left a widower or children. Her photo was in the *Old McGill*, 1914. It showed a blonde, round-faced young woman; the epithet inscribed next to the photo was "I have strange power of speech." She had indeed: she was a linguist and spoke at least five languages, I would later discover.

With a few phone calls I traced her to McGill's German Department, where Professor Trudis Goldsmith said she had known of Marjorie Goldstein but had arrived herself only in 1964, the year before Marjorie died, and had actually never met her. Marjorie, she said, had worked under Professor Bertha Meyer, the chair of the German Department and "something of an institution" who unfortunately had also passed away. She couldn't recall Bertha Meyer ever mentioning Marjorie or Whitehead.

The October 1965 obituaries in the Montreal newspapers gave the names of Marjorie's parents as the late Mr. and Mrs. Jacob Goldstein; there was also a sister in Vancouver, Dorothy, Mrs. M. Grossman. I phoned Ron Finegold at the Jewish Public Library. He found Jacob Goldstein, who had a daughter Marjorie, born in 1893, in a 1926 volume, *The Jews in Canada*. He and his brother were in the tobacco industry; their father had founded Dominion Tobacco, manufacturers of Sweet Caporal cigarettes. Jacob was also a former president of the Temple Emanu-El-Beth synagogue in Westmount—"definitely a well-known and prosperous Jewish family," Finegold said.

Through the synagogue and other sources, I was able to trace relatives of Marjorie. Her sister, a twin, had also passed away, but Dorothy's daughter, Mrs. Janice Grossman Pollack, had memories of her aunt. Through her and cousins in Montreal and Sarasota, Florida, it was possible to piece together a sketch of Marjorie.

She was a large, cultured woman with a passion for literature and music. Besides teaching Spanish and German at McGill, she had been a language teacher for three decades at Trafalgar School for Girls in Montreal. She also gave private tutorials. The Canadian contralto Maureen Forrester took a few lessons with her in pronunciation of Spanish and German in 1950 and 1951, "mostly sitting in the school's library, and once I believe at her house, but I don't remember where it was," said Maureen when I contacted her. Maureen had been twenty-one at the time, and just starting her career. She remembered Marjorie as "a heavy-set woman bursting with energy. I never saw her with a man. I don't know anything about her private life."

One of Marjorie's cousins remembered a man in her life who

answered Whitehead's description. "He was tall and slim. She used to go out for dinner with him, and she would stay out quite late. I think she worked for him." Her other relatives, and some colleagues who were found couldn't remember her with any boyfriends. Her obesity, everyone agreed, was a factor in relations with men. She remained single, a devoted teacher, admired by staff and students at Trafalgar. After she died of cancer in 1965 at age seventy-two, the school named a medallion after her which is awarded each year to the sixth-form student making the most effort in language class.

The photo of Hildred Marjorie Goldstein in the school magazine shows a resolute-looking woman. Sandy Amos, the development officer who had been at Trafalgar for twenty years and had studied Spanish under Marjorie, recalled that "She told marvellous tales. Sometimes she would burst out laughing so hard she would start to drool. She was very conscious about her looks of course. Her obesity was always a big problem for her."

The possibilities of learning more about her were thinning out. It seemed that if there had been anything between her and Whitehead, it had been a private, discreet relationship, one more beclouded facet of his strange, shuttered existence.

18

Sleeping Dog Blues

VANCOUVER, CITY OF RAIN, was bathed in blessed sunshine in early October 1986, as it had been during most of the World's Fair. I spent the first day settling in at a small hotel near Gastown, and enjoying the sunshine and festive atmosphere. In the Vancouver Public Library I checked British Columbia directories for Whitehead listings. The father, Joscelyn Bradbury Whitehead, showed up in Kelowna in the early directories, later in Victoria and then, in the 1940s, in Vancouver. In Kelowna there was a Whitehead whose profession was listed as dental mechanic. Could this be the dental connection of my dream? I was planning to leave the next evening for Kelowna.

In the morning I called Gordon Whitehead's brother, hoping he'd agree to a meeting and that it would be possible to see the photo he had of the Houdini puncher. He seemed vexed that this matter "that took place so long ago" was still being pursued.

Although our earlier conversation had ended congenially enough, this time the octogenarian younger brother crustily declared, "I already told you everything that I know. Why don't you let sleeping dogs lie?"

It had been a sleepless night and I was still under the effects of jetting across the continent, so after I hung up I decided to call right back. I tried to convince him that Houdini's last days, though lived so long ago, were still of importance because he had been such a celebrity. Such research was necessary (I kept on) for any proper biography on Houdini to be written; Gordon's name did come up, I reminded him, in some of the recent Houdini studies, excerpts of which could be sent to him. But the brother said tartly that he had thought things over and would not agree to a meeting about this affair and didn't wish to part with Gordon's photo, or even lend it.

When I mentioned that there was much speculation that Houdini had been the victim of fraudulent mediums, the brother, perturbed, said it was all vicious rumour-mongering.

"My brother must have admired Houdini, if he was going to see him to return a book that he had borrowed, as you told me."

Did he have any idea what the book might have been? Again, he said that he had related everything he knew. Did Gordon have any friends in Montreal who might still be alive and might know more about the incident?

"For instance, I wonder"—forging on—"how this might have affected his life, if he ever spoke to you remorsefully about what took place."

"I told you, my brother was a very private person and didn't communicate his feelings to others very much. I never discussed it with him."

I apologized for asking so many questions, and told him I realized how difficult this must be for him and I was sorry to put him through it, but if he felt that his brother no malice toward Houdini and that the punch was nothing more than an accident, then that is what should be said in the story.

"Houdini was known to make statements about his strength, about how powerful a person he was," said the brother, letting the sentence trail off.

The reaction was much the same when I phoned Gordon Whitehead's sister after I found her number in the Vancouver directory; she was also in her eighties, slightly older than her brother, who must have spoken to her about the punch and the investigation into Gordon's family background since she seemed prepared for the call. She said right off the bat that she found it questionable that one would be contacting people in their eighties to bring up an incident that took place sixty years ago.

"I don't want to discuss it at all."

But gosh, his fists killed a man.

She hung up.

In the Vancouver sunshine the ethical question of all this delving started to take hold. Was I as much an assassin as the Houdini slugger by inter-rogating these old people about this business of long ago which they'd prefer to sweep under the rug? Suppose Gordon was just some sad sack who didn't know his own strength. Or suppose he did have evil intent. Didn't these elderly people have the right to finish their days in peace?

I strolled along Hastings Avenue after the two phone calls. Wouldn't it be, well, kinder to scrap the whole project? How far does one go in pursuit of biographical truths?

I was hungry. I should have phoned the Whiteheads on a full stomach and warmed them up with some quips about the weather rather than plunging right in about their brother's fisticuffs and scaring them off.

I went into McDonald's and had a filet o' fish and hot chocolate. If the project was to be abandoned, I'd have to cut down on expenses. McDonald's and Burger King meals and cheap hotels from now on.

In Gastown, I suddenly recalled Smiley's description of Whitehead's cockiness and arrogance, his impenitence, how he even boasted to the lawyer Harry Cohen, "Oh, it was nothing. Let me show you." That, and Houdini writhing in pain in hospital in Detroit.

I walked into the Hotel Vancouver with Versa's number in hand and found a pay phone next to the coatroom.

Somebody had to bring him to justice.

19

Mabel Starts Singing

BUT THERE WAS TOO MUCH noise. The coat-check lady was yakking away on the coatroom phone. I meandered through the opulent lobby, found a shop selling postcards, and wrote to my son, who had always taken a keen interest in the Houdini story.

"The brother wouldn't talk. Hope Mabel will sing." The postman delivering the card to his tranquil college in Oxford could think what he would.

Upstairs on the convention floor, I found a quieter phone and dialled Mabel/Versa's number. Favery answered.

I wish him a merry Thanksgiving, as it was October 11, Canadian Thanksgiving, and rambled on about happening to be in Vancouver for a family reunion and to look in on the Fair. Would it be possible to get together with himself and Mrs. Greene in the next few days?

He said he didn't think she could add anything to "the situation" and she was still quite upset.

"May I ask why she is so upset over it?" I inquired.

"Well, Gordon never told her anything. She found out about it only after he died."

"How did she find out about it?"

Favery, again in the role of intermediary, transmitted the questions to the hard-of-hearing Versa.

"How did you find out about that situation?" he shouted.

"I don't … remember," Versa could be heard replying in a subdued voice in the background.

"Would it be possible to meet her in person? I'd be willing to write down the questions," I offered.

"He wants to meet you," Favery shouted again. "He'll write out the questions."

"What are the questions?" she could be heard asking in the distance.

"She says she'd prefer if you told her the questions first," Favery said. "Can you tell her now what the questions are?"

"Well, I'm not quite prepared. Well, maybe. Can you ask her to describe Joscelyn physically?"

Favery communicated the question.

"Tall, thin," she replied in a feeble voice.

"What kind of person was he?"

A moment later Favery replied. "She says she never discussed anything with him of his personal, public, and social life."

The conversation continued for a while in this vein. She said that Whitehead had been sick, without specifying what he had other than that he had a gimpy leg which he injured falling down a twenty-five foot hole. The doctors thought he would never walk again, that he would be a paraplegic his whole life, but he got out of the wheelchair, though he had a pronounced limp.

"He had been sick most of his life," she said. But she didn't know how he died, or didn't want to say.

As for Marjorie Goldstein, she was in love with him. Favery added, on behalf of Versa, that when Marjorie saw that Whitehead was not going to get better, "she got up and walked out."

Did Joscelyn have any other friends? He may have, Versa replied, but if so, he never discussed the Houdini situation with them. Why, I asked, did she have such unhappy memories of him? Favery said that it was because of the Houdini thing. Incidentally, Favery added, transmitting a comment from Versa, he always used the name "Gordon" with her. She never knew him as Joscelyn.

How long had she known him? Several years, Favery replied after conferring with Versa.

Had she been in love with him? Favery suggested, in a muffled voice, that she had been, "but it would upset her if I asked that. You must remember, she's an old woman, and it's very trying for her to talk about this."

"Could you ask her if Gordon had any special interests?"

She replied again that she didn't know him that well and didn't discuss private things.

"Was he a mystic?"

Favery seemed to tighten up.

"That isn't something we can discuss. That's a whole different realm."

He asked what Whitehead's birth date was. I told him.

"I don't think he had good relationships. He was probably jealous because other people could get up and go, and he couldn't."

"Because of his limp?"

"You might say so. Certainly," Favery continued with his reading, "he was a highly intelligent person, but sometimes if you're too brilliant you can become egotistical. He was definitely eccentric. He was a graduate from McGill. Whatever he was doing, he must have been jealous, and he showed it."

I sensed that there was something about Whitehead's character or past that Versa and Favery, and the brother too, knew but weren't letting out.

I was planning to leave that evening for Kelowna. Would it be possible to meet Versa later in the week, I asked. Favery said they would think about it. Most likely it would be possible "since you've come such a long way just to see us. Phone when you come back from Kelowna and we'll see what we can arrange."

20

The Okanagan Monster

ONE OF THE "Reasons Why Kelowna is a Desirable Place to Live In" given by the 1922 Wrigley's British Columbia Directory is "good class of people." Kelowna is where Whitehead's father, Joscelyn Bradbury Whitehead, ran a pool hall—"Whitehead's Cigar and Billiards." Was Gordon's character formed in the musty air of his father's pool hall?

Kelowna now has wide avenues, broad pedestrian crosswalks, and clean pretty streets. About 200 miles southeast of Vancouver in the heart of the rich Okanagan Valley, it is a fruit marketing and distribution centre with a mostly prosperous population of 60,000 citizens.

When Joscelyn Gordon Whitehead was growing up there in the early 1900s it was a rough burg. The population in 1909, when he would have turned fourteen, was a mere 1,800. The town had a frontier mentality. Police reports are full of arrests for "drunk and disorderly," "drunk and incapable," and "supplying an interdict with liquor." Wrestling was one of the most popular attractions. Whitehead may even have been in the stands when Al Hatch of Vancouver fought Clarence Eklund, middleweight champion of Canada: "Eklund to Throw Hatch Twice in One Hour—Winner Takes All" goes the headline. Brawls of an extemporaneous nature were even more frequent. The weeklies, *Kelowna Courier* and *Okanagan Orchardist*, regularly carried colourful reports on doings such as a fight between two Russians, one of whom

pled guilty to stabbing his compatriot in the leg with a knife, the act being one of self-defence, he claimed. … The wounded party, a big wild-looking Cossack with a reputation of being a "Buttinsky," was fined $10 for assaulting the knifer and ordered to pay his own doctor's bill. He was quite peeved with the decision after pleading that he was a peace-loving individual, but the Russian interpreter wagged his head and solemnly advised the subject of the Czar to "come through." … He cussed like a drosky driver but dug up the coin.

The town started to prosper when Gordon Whitehead was growing up. "Fruitful in Unity" became its motto. By 1922, the population would balloon to 6,000, and the town boasted four churches, three schools, a hospital, an exhibition building, an opera house, a race track, a roller skating rink, a municipal park with a mile of lake frontage, and daily steamers connecting to Penticton at the other end of the lake.

There were not too many people around who remember the pool room, which no longer existed. But I did manage to touch base with one old-timer, ninety-two-year-old Turner Fumerton, whose family owned a furniture store near Whitehead's Billiards and Cigars. He used to drop in occasionally in the early 1920s to shoot a game because he loved pool. He said the room was in an old wooden building opposite Beven's hardware store. Women weren't permitted inside and many of the town's men made it their second home. Fumerton couldn't recall meeting any of Whitehead's sons there, although he did remember Joscelyn B., the father. He was "a nice fellow. He was interested in photography. I bought a big box camera from him once, paid twenty dollars for it, which was a fortune in those days. I probably still have it some place."

Fumerton's memory of a pool room which he patronized some threescore years earlier was one of the few reasonably interesting pieces of information gleaned during three days in the fruit capital. Otherwise it was mostly, um, fruitless research, riffling through archives at City Hall, the Kelowna Museum, the *Daily Courier* library, churches, and cemeteries, in a quest to find out more about Whitehead's background, and to see what it might have been like growing up there. Most important, perhaps I would find a photograph of him. Nowhere in the Houdini literature is there a picture of the student who walloped the magician.

The fact that I found next to nothing in itself suggests something, if not unsavoury, at least enigmatic about Gordon Whitehead's background. Whitehead père's name showed up on Kelowna voter's lists starting in 1913 up until 1930, his profession given as "Billiard Hall Proprietor." His wife, Gordon's mother Mary Elizabeth Whitehead, appears on the lists as "Housewife." Their address in the 1916 Okanagan Telephone Company directory was given as 204 Burne Avenue; I hired a cab and drove up and down the street, but couldn't find the house. Unless the numbers were changed years ago, it doesn't exist.

There was nothing, anywhere, to be found on Gordon himself. Strangest of all was that his name wasn't on school graduation lists, for according to his McGill card he had graduated from Kelowna High School in 1914. The *Courier* and the *Orchardist* published promotion lists on July 2, 1914 and his name is not there. Nor could he be found in any school board records, although his brothers' and sisters' names show up. It was as if Gordon never existed, or never lived in Kelowna.

I was curious how the weekly papers played up Houdini's death. The big story on November 4, 1926, the first issue to appear after the magician's demise, splashed over front and inside pages, was about the Okanagan's MacIntosh Red being awarded first prize as "the finest dessert apple grown in the British Empire" at the Imperial Fruit Show in London. Not a word on Houdini or Whitehead. The one crime story was about a prison riot at the Tombs in New York which left four dead. And the only piece about Halloween was "Party Draws Big Crowd. Gay Scene at Annual Fancy Dress Event Held by Ladies of Scout Auxiliary."

On my last day there, I was sitting on a bench in the city park facing Okanagan Lake. Maybe because of the dainties sampled at a deli called Jonathan L. Segal's, I was feeling seagullish myself—worldly, mystical, unbound. Ready to fly. Looking at a gossamer mist moving in over the water, I wondered if Whitehead had ever sat here at dusk waiting for the Okanagan monster Ogopogo to rip across the surface. Legend has it that Ogopogo was hatched from long-trapped dinosaur eggs released by movements of the earth's crust. The indigenous Chinook people called Ogopogo the Wicked One and Great Beast of the Lake. They said it had a horse's or goat's head, was well-bearded, and had magic powers which enabled it to escape detection. Maybe Whitehead learned a few tricks from Ogopogo.

While ruminating, I heard someone call my name. I turned around.

In one of those wizardly small-world coincidences, a Québécois acquaintance from my village on the other side of Canada was standing there, young rosy-cheeked (from apple-picking in the sun) Philippe. He had been working on farms all summer and was as surprised as I was to meet someone from tiny Sutton.

21

"My Scary World"

~

BACK IN VANCOUVER I phoned Favery O'Connor. Versa was out and he suggested calling back in the afternoon. She had agreed to meet, he said, either in her apartment or in a restaurant. I suggested it might be easier to at least start in the apartment—we could move to a restaurant later—because if she was hard of hearing we'd have to converse in loud voices and would be overheard by everyone. Favery agreed. He said he wanted to clarify something that came out during our last phone chat. Whitehead wasn't jealous of others due to his limp, he said. He had misunderstood Versa. She had told him, "Gordon had too much character to be jealous."

"What did she mean by this?" I asked.

"You should ask Versa," he suggested.

I called again in the afternoon. Versa was now back, but she was tired, not feeling up to par. Besides, the sixteenth was a bad day for any kind of business, Favery adjudged, because the number carried negative vibrations. He said the vibrations would be much better the next day. "Seventeen is a very good number," he pronounced.

I told him that would be cutting things rather tight because I was scheduled to fly back to Montreal the next evening. Favery suggested we could meet any time tomorrow, "even seven in the morning, if that would suit you". He offered to pick me up at the hotel, dump the luggage in his trunk and serve as chauffeur to the airport after the meeting with Versa. He seemed insistent on doing it this way.

By this time, I must say, I was feeling pervasively paranoid. If they thought that this writer from the east was onto the plot to bump off Houdini, and if Versa through her association with Whitehead and various spiritualists—Favery no doubt was one of them—knew of the

119

conspiracy, wasn't it possible that the writer-who-knew-too-much would be the next cadaver on their Stygian cult exter-mination list? There was something fishy about his overly enthusiastic offer to pick me up and his, "You can dump your luggage in the trunk." Did they know that these suitcases were stuffed with vital notes pertaining to the Houdini "assassination"?

Other paranoid scenarios unfolded in my mind, each one scarier than the last. I wondered if I'd ever see the end of October. Who would be waiting in Versa's living room? It was obvious they had something up their murderous sleeves. I recalled the account given by Houdini murder-plot theorist Norman Bigelow in *Death Blow* of how the spiritualists were trying to get him even as late as 1976. He writes,

> I was told that my theories were not liked, that the Houdini story was nice just the way it is and that it was kept that way for fifty years and would be kept that way for another fifty even if someone had to bury me at Houdini's tomb. I was plagued with threats over the telephone and cars parked outside my house.

I hadn't been threatened, yet. It was more subtle. But if they offered a cup of murky, no doubt deadly nightshade-spiked tea, or canapés made with freshly picked (poisonous) mushrooms, their "treats" would be politely refused. I called Favery and told him thanks anyway but it wouldn't be necessary for him to drive out to the hotel because I'd decided to rent a car "for sightseeing purposes" and would find the Marpole district where Versa lived, without any problem.

"Well, that's up to you," he said. "I could have shown you around."

I called Avis and arranged a car pick-up for the morning, and then I phoned one of the Vancouver uncles. I briefly filled him in on the next day's suicidal research, giving him Versa's address and phone number and said he should alert the police if there was no news from me by five in the afternoon.

Not long after I went to bed that night, I got up again to open the door a crack and check the corridor. Not a soul. I returned to bed, groped for the mini-tape recorder on the commode and, just in case, put out a calling-all-cars paranoid alert:

> To police. This is to inform you that should there be any bloodbath in this room tonight, the person to be questioned is Miss Versa Greene who lives on Fremlin Avenue in Vancouver. Her number and address are in the phone book. That's Greene spelled with an "e". Mr. Favery O'Connor living at the same address should also be investigated in the event of foul play.

There, all bases were covered. I tried sleeping but I couldn't. Morning brought no relief. If anything the shakes were worse, not helped by half a dozen or so Gastown coffees. The meeting was scheduled for ten. At nine-thirty I phoned Favery to announce that the alarm didn't go off and I was running a little late. He was wrong about the vibrations: the seventeenth was even worse than the sixteenth. Trying to find the Marpole district, I took a wrong turn somewhere after the Cambie Bridge and drove alongside something that looked like the Great Wall of Vancouver splashed with a huge white-painted grafitti message—"IT'S A SCARY WORLD!"

By 10:30 I had found Fremlin, a tree-lined residential street with nondescript two-storey apartment houses on either side. Versa's was no different than the others. I drove around the block several times, ensuring that there wasn't anyone vicious, violent, or vituperative lurking in front of the building. I kept glancing in the rear-view mirror to see if anyone mediumistic-looking was tailgating. After ascertaining no one was in pursuit, I parked several blocks away just in case they'd hired someone to pry open the trunk and steal the precious Houdini files. Before getting out, I recorded a new alert:

> To police officers. I am now going into 8[…] Fremlin, Apartment 101 to meet Miss Versa Greene and Favery O'Connor about Harry Houdini. Should anything happen to me, or should I not come back to this car, they are the people who should be questioned. Repeat. 8[…] Fremlin Avenue, Apartment 101. Versa Greene lived with Joscelyn Gordon Whitehead who died in 1954 and was the gentleman

who delivered the punch to Houdini in 1926 that resulted nine days later in Houdini's death. Mr. Whitehead has not been heard from since. I have tracked him down after years of meticulous research, much of which is in the suitcase in the trunk of this car.

More files on this case can be found at my home in Sutton, Quebec. [Street number given], postal code Joe Two KO, or Joe Two-Knockouts. We live in a colony of First Nations boxers. The name of my ex-wife is [...]. My son Daniel is studying at Oxford, England, my daughter Valerie is living in Jamaica. Their addresses are [...]. In Vancouver here I have an uncle [name, address, and phone number given]. And another uncle who lives with him [name given]. Miss Greene and Mr. O'Connor may be extremely dangerous and may be members of a bizarre spiritualist cult. This may be a trap I'm walking into. Another person who is on this trail is Norman Bigelow. B-i-g-e-l-o-w, in Fitchburg, Massachusetts. His address is in one of the files in the trunk of this car. He is a person who would be very interested in this research. Should anything happen to me, whatever earthly belongings I possess shall be equally divided between my son Daniel and daughter Valerie. This codicil supersedes all other previous last wills and testaments.

Click.

On the front passenger side of the rented car, on top of the tape recorder, I left a note, written in large felt-pen letters, addressed to the police:

POLICE: If not back and this car seems abandoned, listen to last few minutes of this cassette tape.
　　Don Bell, Oct. 17/86.
　　10:30 a.m.

I opened the door, half expecting a shot would ring out. As I approached Versa's building a man with swabbed hair and a pink elfish face came out of the door, holding out his paw.

"Hello, Mr. Bell. I'm Favery O'Connor. We're waiting for you."

22

Versa Breaks Down

VERSA WAS A DOLLOP of a lady with large shiny hazel eyes and a puggish nose. She looked as if she'd tip over if a draft blew in. But I was still on guard. There was something familiar about her, as if I'd met her somewhere recently. Or was it because she resembled someone? She was wispy-looking, delicate, quiet at first, letting Favery O'Connor, her up-front man, do all the talking, as he had on the phone.

He looked as though he might have stepped out of an Irish pub. He wore a loose-fitting faded jacket, a plain white shirt open at the collar, and under it a T-shirt which curled around a thick dockworker's neck.

"I'm making a pot of coffee," Favery said, as he steered me to a large soda in the living room facing Versa, who was in an armchair, her back to the window. "Or would you prefer tea?"

"Geez, I'm up to my eyeballs in coffee." No doubt it was prepared with the special "magical" beans. One sip and …

"Thanks anyway."

"Water?"

"Oh, I'm fine."

The apartment was comfortably decorated, middle-class senior-citizen-like, quite ordinary, except for a framed picture on top of the bookshelf which seemed out of place, a portrait of a guru-ish looking occidental man in Indian attire, lotus-positioned on cushion.

"You found us easily enough?" Favery asked.

"Oh, sure, no problem."

"Where did you park?"

"Down the street."

"You could have parked right in front."

"Oh—" stumbling, "I thought it was just for residents."

Versa had her eyes fixed on me.

Suddenly, I realized where I had seen her. She was the Vancouver clone of my québécoise ex-mother-in-law. She was about the same size and age, and had similar features and the same delicate frame. I suddenly had the eerie feeling that I was talking to Madame Dubé in her kitchen in Outremont, ready to accuse her of palsy-walsying around with a murderer.

"How can we help you?" asked Favery?

Not knowing where to start, I handed Versa some sheets with questions about Whitehead and the Houdini affair. "I prepared these questions last night," I said, speaking loud because of her hearing problem. "We could just talk but this will at least give you an idea of the kind of information that—" I looked at Favery for reassurance.

"What would you like to know about Gordon?" she asked in a sweet voice, almost a whisper.

"Whatever you can remember. Whatever you would like to tell me."

Versa slowly read the first of the three handwritten pages, paused, went on to the second. "He had an expansive mind," she said. To one question, she replied, "Oh, that I don't know. I don't remember. That was before I knew him." To another: "That was a part of his life I didn't know anything about."

"He was very secretive," Versa said when she reached the bottom of the second page. Her voice was faltering.

"He was unique," she added.

"In what way?"

Suddenly, Versa's body began to quiver and she burst into tears. I looked to Favery for help. He tried comforting her. "It's all right, Versa, we won't talk about Gordon now." He went behind and started rubbing her shoulders.

"I'm sorry," I offered, suddenly feeling ashamed to be putting her through this.

"It's not your fault," Favery said, speaking in a whisper. "Even though it was long ago, she was deeply attached to Gordon. It's still difficult for her to talk about him, and even more so since she found out about the Houdini thing."

Versa Greene, 1986. She knew the man who punched Houdini at the
Princess Theatre, October 22, 1926.
Photo by Don Bell

He gently sculpted her shoulders, trying to relax her. To change the subject, we talked about numerology and cures for asthma. Favery had been up half the night preparing a thirty-seven page plan of action for me which involved using herbs like lobelia, going on a strict vegetarian diet and eating lots of lemons. Dark forces? So far, naught. He handed me the handwritten plan and suggested reading it after returning to Quebec and explained that its acceptance and payment of fifty dollars was on the condition that the treatment not be discussed with other people, especially doctors.

I asked him if Favery was his real name. His original name, the name his parents chose, he said, was Francis Nelson. But he wanted a V and a Y in his name. He considered Avery, than added an F and it became Favery, which was an obscure Irish given name. There was also a "very" in Favery, which was a good omen. Versa also wanted a V name, he said. She chose Versa on a whim after finding a Styrofoam coffee cup which was marked Versa, "possibly the name of a company".

She came originally from Cheshire in England, Favery said. "And she's just like a cheshire cat." Versa, now calmer, heard him and laughed at this. "Isn't that right, Versa? Just like a cheshire cat." Favery said he used to be a private chauffeur in New York. He was from New Jersey originally. Versa knew his parents. He left the rat race, drove west, and settled in Seattle. Then he looked Versa up in Vancouver. And here he was. He had a warm, close relationship with her. He took her out, watered her plants ...

Favery saw that I had noticed the portrait on top of the bookshelf.

"That's Eugene Fersen." He was the founder, Favery explained, of a movement called "The Fundamental Science of Being", which tried to answer questions about the immutable laws of the universe, where we are going and why. Fersen had been Versa's spiritual teacher and guide for forty years. Versa reached for a leaflet on the table next to her which described the lessons that could be bought, lessons which opened up the individual to development on the mental, physical, and spiritual planes. Under the mental plane (mind), Lesson Eleven, I noticed, was called "The Solar Plexus—Its Storehouse". Was there some relation between this and the Houdini punch and Whitehead?

I inched again into a conversation about Whitehead. Had he been a follower of Fersen? Versa said she wanted him to be, but he was skeptical and didn't seem open to Fersen's teachings, but she never really talked to him much about the Science of Being, although "Gordon was a very spiritual person," she said. She quivered again now that the conversation had switched back to Whitehead.

"We can go to the restaurant now," I suggested.

"Yes, that would be a good idea," agreed Favery.

Before leaving the apartment, Favery handed me a pamphlet published by The Lightbearers of Seattle, Washington which, on the cover, showed a strange angelic-looking man clad entirely in blue whose torso emitted a golden light. Under the portrait was written, "THE MORNING STAR—The Picture with a Soul". It was considered the masterpiece of Princess M. Eristoff, a Russian artist, and, according to the pamphlet,

was painted during the first years of the Great War, at the request of Baron Eugene Fersen, of Moscow, Russia, its present owner—

No coverings guard his feet from the sharp stones that strew his path, or blunt the keen fangs of heat and cold and storms; yet his steps do not falter; he moves tranquilly on, strong in the knowledge of his mission.

Favery's car was parked in front. We drove to a Chinese restaurant in a nearby shopping mall. There, a chatty Hungarian waitress moved from table to table. Versa was now smiling and seemed glad to be out of the house, as if she was on a date, being treated. "She doesn't step out that often," Favery commented. Versa ordered a toasted cheese sandwich and fries, asking the waitress for a doggy bag for the fries, and a half coffee, half hot water. Favery had a Spanish omelet which he sprinkled copiously with a jigger of his own cayenne pepper which he always carried.

Now that we were fed—and in spite of my having to shout because of her hearing problem—Versa slowly warmed up to talking about Whitehead. I guessed that she had been deeply in love with him, and, as she had apparently been a spinster her whole life, Whitehead may have been her one big love.

"But it was all so long ago, and I don't remember much," she said.

23

The Man Who Punched Houdini

HE DIDN'T TAKE CARE of himself, said the woman who loved him and who buried him. He was thin as a reed, sick, troubled, malnourished. He was in a coma when she saw him last, in the Queen Elizabeth Hospital in Montreal. He was a secretive, strange person. She knew him over a few years at the end of his life. She was giving special eye exercise courses which she learned in New York, the Bates method. Whitehead dropped in on her one day when she was living on MacKay, then continued dropping in. But he already knew Marjorie Goldstein and was staying with her some of the time. Versa brought him baskets of fruit and vegetables when he was sick, leaving them at his door or at Marjorie's. She didn't know whether he ate them or not. He stayed with Marjorie, although he kept his own apartment on Lincoln.

He was a very special person, Versa continued. There was much that he could have given the world. He was intelligent, knew just about everything, but didn't take care of himself. He was self-conscious about his limp. He fell twenty-five feet off some scaffolding while working in construction.

She knew some people from Sutton—Dorothy and Morton Jaquays. Whitehead took her to a lecture Morton Jaquays gave on Dianetics. The Jaquays said if she ever needed them she could stay with them in Sutton. They ran Paramount Farms Bakery and were involved in alternative philosophies and various spiritual movements, including Subud, the mystic movement founded in the 1930s by a Javanese who called himself Pak Subuh. His real name was Muhammad Subuh Sumohadiwidjojo. He preached a principle known as Latihan whereby subjects are "opened" by submitting themselves to the life force transmitted to them by the

Versa Greene and her friend, the numerologist Favery O'Conner.
Photo by Don Bell

Subud teacher.

She had a breakdown after Gordon died. She was shattered. "My life fell to bits and pieces." She spent a year and a half convalescing on the Jaquay's farm, by coincidence, about two kilometres from my residence.

I later managed to track down Mort Jaquays Jr., the eldest son of Mort senior and his first wife, in Montreal. He didn't remember anyone named Whitehead, or a man matching his description, staying at the farmhouse in Sutton. He was about fifteen when Mabel arrived at his parents' house to recover after Whitehead died. He remembered her as "a smallish mousy woman who hung out for quite some time." She may have been attracted to them because his father and his father's new wife Dorothy "were playing around with some oddball eastern religions at the time."

"In the early 1950s my father was also up to his neck in Dianetics, the precursor of Scientology. He even went down to Arizona to visit its founder L. Ron Hubbard. It was a self-help psychology sort of thing, not related to spiritualism, but it might have interested Mabel."

At a meeting at Cours Mont-Royal in Montreal I showed him the photo of Gordon Whitehead. "No," he said, "he doesn't look familiar. But this could have happened without my knowing about them. I wasn't always there. I was at boarding school in the late 1940s, if that's when the photo was taken.

"I haven't the faintest idea how she [Mabel] happened to arrive at the house. I know she just arrived one day and moved in and became a fixture. She definitely wasn't a friend of my mother's. She came possibly through my father, or through Dorothy, or one of the hangers-on. She was very quiet, withdrawn. I don't remember any spark to her. My memory is quite visual, but I can't remember anything about her that stands out, nor any stories around the table about Houdini."

Thirty-two years after Whitehead died Versa still trembled when she thought of him. "I miss him. I still do … miss him." Her voice trailed off. She took nerve pills. She came to Vancouver three years ago, perhaps hoping to forget, but she regretted it and now felt stuck here. She had some friends, but they were gone and now there was only Favery to take care of her.

She believed in reincarnation. Whitehead and Marjorie Goldstein were her parents in another life. She was their only child. When she was in their apartment, "I felt something. It's hard to explain. I just know." Was he unbalanced? He was psychic. He was eccentric. Was he involved in spiritualism? "I wouldn't know anything about that."

He never talked to her about the Houdini blows. It was only after he died that she found out.

"I can't tell you much more," she said. She started to sob again. "I thought I should see you because you're going to so much trouble for your book. He was so gifted. It was so tragic."

Favery suggested it was the curse of his name. The "J" of Joscelyn suggests someone out in left field. "You can't change the vibration of your name. You're stuck with it, until you change your name, and even then it takes a year for the vibration of the new name to assume itself." The waitress who heard all this (she too, she said, was born in Vienna, like Houdini) brought Versa's takeout bag with the fries and we left. The world wasn't as scary a place as it was before, but there were still question marks about the man who punched Houdini.

"We enjoyed your visit," said Favery.

"I enjoyed it too. We'll keep in touch, won't we?"

"Yes, I hope your asthma feels better. You will find the treatment that's been prescribed, if you follow it exactly, will bring considerable relief."

They posed for photos in front of the apartment. Favery the herbalist and helpmate, and saintly Versa, sweetly looking into the camera. "Please send us a copy of your book when it comes out, won't you?" asked Favery. We shook each other's hands. I kissed Versa on both cheeks. Goodbye, goodbye.

24

The Big Break

A PHONE CALL from Paris from writer Gérald Robitaille—another lucky coincidence—set in motion events that led to the discovery of someone else who knew the elusive Whitehead and who also, miracle or miracles, had what every Houdini scholar for the last sixty years has been trying to find, a photograph of J. Gordon Whitehead.

Robitaille (now deceased) moved from Montreal to Paris in 1953, influenced by Henry Miller's free-hearted philosophy and voluptuous writings. He befriended the dirty old genius, and starting in 1967 Gérald and his wife Diane lived with Miller for two years in Pacific Palisades, California. Gérald worked as Henry's private secretary (out of which evolved his controversial portrait *Le Père Miller*, which Anaïs Nin thought was too personal and should have been toned down).

I had written several articles about Robitaille's amitié with Miller. We became friends and kept in touch. So in the spring of 1988, Gérald called from Paris asking for help with some paperwork regarding his application for a Canadian government pension. A week later he sent a letter with a list of addresses where he had at one time or another lived in Montreal. One was on Mackay, where he resided from 1951 to 1953—right next door to Mabel Jackson.

When I wrote back with the pension information, I filled Gérald in on the Houdini project and asked if by any chance he had known either Whitehead or Mabel.

"Yes, the name 'J.G. Whitehead' does mean something, but very vague," he replied in a letter written June 27, 1988,

Mabel Jackson too. It was Archie Handel's brother-in-law, an Englishman married to his sister who was my neighbour on rue Mackay, who had spoken of them, and it seems I had met them in his bookstore, in front of Everyman's on Ste. Catherine. But really your letter évoque un rêve! Archie still has his store—Diamond Bookstore on Sherbrooke near Vendôme. You could look him up and from there, his brother-in-law. Go ahead, Sherlock!

Across the street from Everyman's Bookstore? Of course: Rodick's bookstore, on the south side of Ste. Catherine close to Mackay two blocks from Sam Smiley's office. A wonderful depository of second-hand books, it had closed down in the 1960s around the same time that the CBC/ Radio Canada had moved out of the old Ford Hotel nearby on Dorchester (now boulevard René Lévesque) to its new headquarters on Dorchester East. Jack and Frances Rodick knew their books inside out. They carried general stock, but also old and rare books on religion and mysticism. Maybe Whitehead had been a customer.

I phoned Archie Handel. Yes, he said, his sister Frances and brother-in-law Jack are still around, now in their early seventies, retired, and living in Westmount. He passed on their phone number and I called.

Jack answered, a familiar voice though the last time we had spoken had been in the store fifteen or twenty years earlier. I told him about the Houdini project and asked if he knew Whitehead. He said, "Why don't you drop by tomorrow morning?"

At eleven o'clock the next morning, August 24, 1988, I rang the bell at their house on a quiet street in lower Westmount. Jack, a fit-looking soft-spoken man with just a trace of English accent (he was born in Wallasey in Merseyside), opened the door. He seemed not to have changed a whit from his bookstore days. Frances was upstairs but would come down soon, he said. We went into the kitchen; he poured some coffee, I set up the tape recorder and we started talking.

Yes, he had met Whitehead, Rodick said, although he didn't know him well. He didn't know much about him personally.

"He used to come into our shop to buy a book occasionally, usually in the evenings. It would have been in our early years, probably in the later forties or early fifties, in the old shop, which we opened in 1947, before we moved next door on Ste. Catherine—our Gypsy blood! He always came around by himself.

"I remember that he wore a dark raincoat and what you call a fedora hat but in England they call a trilby. I seem to recall that he had a slight English accent, as if he was born in England or educated there, or at least brought up in an English family environment. He seemed well educated, spoke very well, was extremely polite, and he was cultured—in the sense of culture being something cultivated, like it had been developed in the ground and nurtured.

"We stayed open until ten o'clock in those days. Many of our customers came in an hour or so before closing, often just to talk about books or to socialize. A bookshop isn't like a supermarket or a department store. It's a place where people gather and exchange ideas, and our customers, especially in the evening, came in for that.

"After locking up, we'd usually go to Murray's Restaurant a few doors away on Ste. Catherine Street with the last few customers of the night and the conversations would continue over coffee and cake. Murray's stayed open until eleven then, mostly to get people in from Her Majesty's Theatre [located nearby on Guy Street] after the shows. It was too late for a full meal, but they still served desserts and coffee and tea.

"I don't remember that much about the topics we discussed with Whitehead—it would have been thirty or thirty-five years ago—except that he did tell us, once, probably in Murray's, that he knew Houdini and that he was the one that was involved.

"The way he related it, it was if it was a sad, kind of irresponsible, incident. If I tried to tell you details about what he said, in all fairness I might be confusing it with things I read in a magazine. He certainly wasn't boasting about it then. I don't think he felt proud of having hit Houdini. Perhaps at the time of the incident he might have had such feelings. He might have been brash as young students sometimes are [although Whitehead was thirty-one when he hit Houdini] and then later on would have felt it wasn't such a smart thing to do. Hopefully, people mature.

"He gave the impression," Rodick recalled, "of someone who read a lot. It's too far back to remember the kind of books he bought from us.

Books on spiritualism? I would just be taking a guess. I kind of remember that he was slightly bent, as people who do a lot of studying can become, bent at the shoulder. He never looked very healthy, in fact, I seem to recall that he had a slight skin imperfection, not spots or lumps but as if there was a faint rash somewhere on his skin. It's perhaps why we never saw him without his long coat. Wait a moment."

Jack got up and left the kitchen. He returned with a manila envelope, which he opened. He pulled out a photograph.

"I thought this would interest you."

"That's—?"

"Whitehead. The one on the right, with the coat and the trilby."

"My God!"

The man who punched Houdini suddenly became a flesh-and-blood creature. The long jaw, the shabby overcoat, the bent-brimmed hat, the big hands that once knitted into a fist and killed the magic. To say that it produced goose bumps would be an understatement.

"It was taken in our old shop. It must have been some time between 1947 when we opened and 1954, if that was when he died. I would guess around 1950. The other fellow," Rodick pointed out, "is Maurice Whitbread, an Englishman who happened to be in the store when I took the photo. He was ambitious to be a writer and eventually worked for us, not for long, then returned to England. He must have known Whitehead but I don't know how well they knew each other. Whitehead and Whitbread!" the bookman chuckled. "Like a team in vaudeville."

While we were studying the photograph: "He looks like Tyrone Power in *The Sun Also Rises*, don't you think?" Jack asked.

Frances came down; she too seemed hardly to have changed over the years.

Yes, she also had memories of Gordon Whitehead—"a fragile-looking, tragic-looking man," as she described him. She remembered that "he always came into the store late at night.

"And then he told us his story. I think that really haunted him," Frances stated.

"Haunted him?"

"Oh, yes."

The only known photo of J. Gordon Whitehead (wearing hat) in Rodick's
Bookstore, Montreal, circa 1950 with Maurice Whitbread,
who would eventually work in the store.
Photo by Jack Rodick

Did she remember what prompted him to tell them about his involvement with Houdini?

"I can't really say. People in bookstores, of course, usually speak about books. Perhaps it was after he had ordered some books from us? And perhaps, not unnaturally, he had a special interest in Houdini. We did sell a lot of books on Houdini. He may even have asked us to order a Houdini book. I can't really recall."

She agreed with her husband that the conversation about Houdini must have taken place at Murray's after they had closed the bookstore for the night.

"At the store, we heard thousands of stories, usually in bits and pieces. Some people we never saw again. They'd drop in and unburden themselves. We'd have to serve a customer or answer the phone and they'd walk through the door. But when we were in Murray's it was a different atmosphere, there were no interruptions, so I'm quite sure it must have been there if we can still remember him telling us about it.

"Sometimes," she recalled, "we were with a crowd in Murray's, sometimes just one. And I think he was just one at the time. I doubt that he would have confided in us, not something like that, if there had been other people at the table.

"When he told us about his involvement in punching Houdini, I didn't like him very much for it. I didn't think he intended what happened, but he wanted to show Houdini up. Like 'Is that what you think? Then I'll show you!' And of course he did hit him. What happened was because Houdini wasn't prepared. Houdini said he couldn't be hurt because he would flex himself and harden his stomach, and he may have said, 'I dare you,' but he hit him at once. Anyway, that's the way I remember the story. Do people remember it differently? Didn't you think he was very unhappy about this?" she asked her husband.

"I felt," Jack Rodick said, as he had before his wife came downstairs, "that as a student he might have been brash about this sort of escapade, but afterwards he didn't seem at all proud of it."

"It's true, he certainly didn't have any sense of bravado about it," she agreed, "not at the time we knew him, but I imagine he was aggressive as a young man.

"He looked disturbed, I thought. I felt he was a very sad man. I really did. I didn't think he told people about the incident very often. He may have been worried about them checking him. And it was just at that one time that he told us, perhaps because he trusted us and knew that we wouldn't be judging him. People tell a lot of things to strangers that they don't tell to intimates, and usually it goes no further. When it happened, perhaps he felt not only that he would be judged, but perhaps even considered guilty of a crime. Houdini was loved, you know, very much so.

"He never told us anything else about himself," she continued. "It was just that one time. And then as quickly as we saw him, he seemed to disappear. We didn't see him for years at a time. Did he travel? Where did he go? Certainly it seemed as if he was a loner. I don't remember whether he worked. Did he work, Jack? To me, he looked too ill. He looked way older than his years, wasted, very pale, very much like in the photograph. And he always wore that overcoat or a gabardine trench coat. Even in the summer he'd be covered up.

"Whitehead may have felt like he committed a terrible crime. We may have been the only people he discussed it with, other than with his family, and even then, did he discuss it with them? I certainly sensed a deep sadness, and it was probably what made him ill. That might have made him mentally ill, I never thought of that, but it's possible, poor man.

"Didn't he imply," Frances asked her husband, "that he was once a very strong man? That I remember clearly. Not his exact words. I thought he was in athletics. I don't remember him ever saying he was a divinity student. I remember his hands, though. They were very large. I think it shows in the photograph. Very large strong hands. I notice hands.

"Why did he come to Montreal," she asked. "To go to McGill? Bad luck for Houdini. And bad luck for himself."

Later in the fall I was in Paris on other business and showed the photo to Gerald Robitaille.

"I have to be honest," Gerald said. "I don't exactly recognize him, but the whole thing somehow gives me a strong feeling of déjà vu. I

Jack and Frances Rodick, 1988.
Whitehead would occasionally drop by their bookstore.
Photo by Don Bell

probably ran into him two or three times in the store. But you know how it is in a bookstore, you say a few words to whoever happens to be in there browsing, you don't really remember them and probably will never see them again. But it's not an unknown face. The other guy looks familiar too. The whole thing is familiar somehow. Presque quarante ans, mon Dieu, comment est-ce que tu veux que je me souviens?

"But when you wrote to me about this," Robitaille continued, "it was especially his name that came back to me because I remembered meeting someone named Whitehead at Rodick's at the time I was reading Bertrand Russell, who mentioned Alfred North Whitehead, the philosopher. I didn't go up to this guy and ask him if he was the cousin of the philosopher, but the name stuck. Don't forget, I'm a French Canadian, fascinated by English names, and when I heard 'Whitehead', I thought, not Roundhead, and not tête carrée—square head," Gerald laughed, "as we call the English."

A French woman, a psychotherapist who worked with troubled children, happened to be in the café when we were having this conversation. She had been looking at the photo while we were talking. She didn't know from beans who Whitehead was. What was her impression of the man with the long coat and the trilby hat in the bookstore photo?

"Il a la gueule de quelqu'un qui méprise les autres," was her impromptu reply—roughly, he has the mug of someone contemptuous of others.

The Rodicks, gentle people themselves, saw genteelness and sadness in Whitehead, but others, as I would soon discover, detected a meaner spirit.

25

The Millers and the Architect

I SHOULD EXPLAIN: that French psychotherapist who was in the café with Robitaille, his wife, and me, was in fact my charming soon-to-be wife. Hence the comings and goings between Paris and Quebec. But in spite of the geographical confusion, in 1990 Houdini was very much on the agenda.

The upstairs neighbour mentioned by Dr. Joseph Scales turned up. Ivie Miller was ninety-two years old and his mind was crisp as a bell. His family had lived on the third floor of the Grove Apartments for a long time, and he was one of several persons who replied to a letter to the editor in the Montreal *Gazette* on December 8, 1990. It called on any old-timers who saw Houdini's performance in Montreal or who knew the student involved in the punching incident to write to my Paris address.

Before jumping into Ivie Miller's letters and the meetings with him, his wife, and their daughters, who all knew Whitehead and compared him to someone out of a macabre Edgar Allan Poe tale, let's consider Richard Bolton.

Among those who responded to the *Gazette* feeler, besides Ivie Miller, was retired Montreal architect Richard Bolton, age eighty-three. He wrote that he knew Whitehead at McGill. Other than Sam Smiley, this was the first person who actually placed Whitehead at McGill at the time of the Houdini blow.

He sent two letters, the second after I wrote asking for more details regarding points he made in the first. A few months later we met in his Westmount apartment. A spry, good-looking widower with all his marbles obviously together, Bolton was well known in the architectural field in Quebec. He was a partner at Fetherstonehaugh Durnford Bolton and Chadwick, served at one time as president of Quebec's Association of Architects, and was Chancellor of the College of Fellows of the Royal Architectural Institute of Canada. "Enough details," he wrote, "for you to make your own judgments as to my reliability. I'm mentally competent and still drive my own car."

He wrote that he met Whitehead around the beginning of 1925 while studying at McGill.

> He was a few years older than many of us, about 6'2" tall, with fair hair and pink complexion, with an accent indicating a British public school education. I don't know when he came to Montreal, but one could expect to see him in 'polite society' and at academic and literary events.
>
> One summer day in 1926, I was looking for a crew for my 27-foot sailboat on Lake St. Louis and a friend (probably Desmond Massey-Beresford) suggested I ask Gordon, who was living alone and was delighted to get out of the town for the day. He was a bit clumsy in a boat and inexperienced but we had a good time. He must have been to our home in Westmount at least once. After I left McGill we lost touch with each other.

When we met, I asked the architect if he could remember any other details about that outing on the lake, which might give some indication of Whitehead's state of mind, since it was so close to the time he had his encounter with Houdini. He recalled,

> It was a beautiful summer day. We arrived at Pointe Claire on the Lakeshore where the boat was moored. Gordon certainly wasn't familiar with this type of boat and it took some time to explain things. We got the sail covers off and I remember there were these bits of odd marlin hanging around. He stopped whatever he was doing and said, "Oh, I never miss an opportunity to pick up and stow away small bits of string, they can be so useful."
>
> I had some forebodings, but I said, okay, there are more important

Retired architect, Richard Bolton, 1991. He met Whitehead in
1925 while studying at university.
Photo by Don Bell.

things to do. When we were out on the lake, it started to blow very, very hard. We were way up around Ile Perrot, a mile from the nearest shore. I realized that we would have to get the mainsail down and shorten it with the bunch of little ropes along the bottom which you cluster together and then hoist it up again. Well, in the process of getting the sail up, with Gordon sort of fooling around down below trying to retrieve these bits of string, we had got it up on the wrong side of another line and it jammed and wouldn't come down.

We anchored and I had to go up the mast, but I couldn't free the sail because it was moving so fast and I couldn't get my knife out of my belt to cut it free. I remember going down at the bottom, pulling the knife out, putting it in my mouth and climbing back up, but I finally got it through. Gordon, who was still gathering the marlin, said, "Well, now, isn't this an exciting kind of thing?" I wasn't feeling at all like I was enjoying the excitement. It was aggravating and it could have been humiliating and very uncomfortable if we had capsized. When I got down I was so exhausted I just heaved my meal over the side.

But we finally got underway and had a nice day. He was a bit of a kook. Very much an oddball he was!

Bolton doubted that his friend of 1926 was the kind of person who would have delivered such a blow, or blows. This was his reason for writing. He was surprised when I told him in my reply that there were witnesses and affidavits and there certainly seemed no question about Whitehead being in Houdini's dressing room.

In his first letter he wrote, "He was in some ways a social misfit, perhaps a bit pedantic. On the other hand I have no idea of Gordon's beliefs or interest in spiritualism and do not know if he could have reacted strongly to Houdini's scorn of spiritualist mediums."

In his follow-up letter he wrote,

There is little I can say except that [the witnesses] were drunk or managed to pin the action on a rather odd fellow who was accustomed to being mocked and bullied and could not think of how to extricate himself. … History is full of faked evidence and this event has that sort of smell. As you can see, I am not convinced, but perhaps I am the gullible one.

In defence of the witnesses, it's hard to imagine that young Sam Smiley drawing Houdini's portrait at eleven in the morning, or his pal Jacques Price, were under the influence. Could they have pinned something on Whitehead? According to the Rodicks, Whitehead confessed that he was in the dressing room and was the one "who was involved."

In his letters Bolton also told of being in the audience at the McGill Union Ballroom. He seemed to remember Whitehead being there too. Houdini enthralled the audience, Bolton recalled, as he lashed out against the mediums.

He was campaigning against belief in physical manifestations by spirits or at spiritualist sessions, claiming that voices, bell-ringing, table movements were fakes. He claimed to be able to reproduce, by illusionist means, any phenomenon which the spiritualist operators could produce. He entertained the audience with conjuring tricks such as making objects disappear and re-appear, by sewing through his cheek, swallowing some beads and bringing up a string of beads on the thread. He showed us how to slip his foot out of a shoe and ring a bell with his toes.

Bolton said that after the lecture there was "a short scuffle" as Houdini prepared to leave the Ballroom.

I could not see clearly because there was a large crowd and we were all standing. I was about thirty feet away. Houdini and the official party, whoever they were, left immediately. A few minutes later somebody told me that a student had punched Houdini in the abdomen. … I seem to remember Whitehead being closer to Houdini than I was when the platform party left the room and the scuffle occurred. But it was all so long ago. What I seem to remember

DON BELL

may only be what I heard about later.

In his second letter, he was even less sure of what he had seen. He recalled Whitehead had

a funny, loping way of walking and I still picture him crossing the room where the Houdini lecture took place but to be honest, it may have been a similar crowd of people in another place. ... If [Professor Tait] was there and said there was no scuffle, then I think he is more credible than my memory of a scuffle. I ... may have seen a stumble or other unrelated event. I did not recognize anyone except Houdini in the area where it took place and I did not see a blow being landed.

Amazingly, more than six decades after attending the magician's lecture, Richard Bolton still remembered a bit of doggerel by the late John Glassco which appeared in the *McGill Daily* at the time:

Thousands saw the great Houdini
Masses shouted for the Queenie
Did you ever see such asses
As the educated masses!

The "Queenie" was the Queen of Rumania who visited Montreal a few days after Houdini.

When I eventually visited Richard, I asked if he could remember anything else about Whitehead that might tie in with the Houdini incident: his behaviour, his friends, what circles he frequented.

"I used to see him at some of the social events that young men were invited to in those days," he told me. "I can remember him at the Ritz Carlton Hotel, at a dance there. Again, this funny, slightly stooped approach, so that his back went that way and his tailcoat hung straight down, an awkward kind of thing. He wasn't terribly upright.

"He had some friends but they weren't friends of mine. I can't recollect any particular women in his life, which was why," the architect noted, "I was interested in your comment about those two girls [Mabel

146

Jackson and Marjorie Goldstein] who were competing for his affection. Although he was an eccentric by the conformist standards of the time, there was never any question about him being anything other than heterosexual, not at the time I knew him, although it was not the kind of thing one talked about in those days. You have to remember he was quite a bit older than we were and the women friends he would have had probably would have been older than the girls I was going around with. We did have some students who were veterans whose education had been interrupted by the Great War and returned to their studies when it was over."

Was Whitehead a veteran? He would have been nineteen when World War I broke out in 1914. The National Archives in Ottawa responded to my inquiry that "from the information provided, we have been unable to identify the above-mentioned as having served in the Canadian Expeditionary Force during World War I."

"I picture him," concluded Bolton at our meeting, "in amongst the somewhat professorial literary types, many of whom came from other places, Scotland, South Africa. Yes, I see him in that milieu. In 1927 I left for Massachusetts Institute of Technology and moved into a very different world, returning to Montreal in 1930, but I don't recall ever seeing Gordon again. But even had he remained, I doubt that we would have met very often or had much in common."

Where Whitehead lived and what he did from the time of the Houdini event until the early 1950s isn't clear. In 1952 we see his name popping up in the Montreal *Lovell's City Directory*. He is living in the Grove Apartments, 1615 Lincoln, Number 11A. Living on the fourth floor in Number 17, is Ivie Miller with his wife Etta and their daughters Doreen and Audrey. A Scotsman like Whitehead, Miller had been an R.A.F. pilot and had worked as manager of a trading station in Nigeria for ten years. Then he worked in the accounting department of Sun Life Insurance in Montreal until his retirement, although he didn't know Mabel Jackson.

Ivie sent two letters and I interviewed him and his wife in their Benny Park apartment in the Notre-Dame-de-Grâce district of Montreal. I also met with their daughter Doreen Turner in St. Hubert on Montreal's

South Shore, and reached their daughter Audrey Searcy in Illinois.

Ivie Miller's first letter began, "I am an ancient, dilettante, short story writer myself and I sympathize with your need and, since I have the information I am happy to pass it on."

After describing a performance by Houdini that he had once witnessed at the Coliseum in Glasgow, Miller moved on to the subject of Whitehead. He was, he wrote, "an extremely private person who invariably discussed nothing of a personal nature. That he had a refined background was obvious."

Like Richard Bolton, Ivie Miller clearly didn't know that the "refined background" included his father's poolroom in Kelowna. As part of his ruse, Whitehead told Ivie that he had studied medicine at McGill, just as he told Houdini that he was a divinity student. Ivie was also led to understand that Whitehead's father had been British Consul in either Hong Kong or Singapore or Shanghai.

During Whitehead's student days, there was an occasion when, working as a hired hand at the construction of the Shawinigan Power and Light Company, a beam fell and struck him on the head, necessitating that implant of a metal plate to his skull. That no doubt ended his student days and in the hiatus until I met him there is no record, unless he was doing what he was doing when I met him at the end of that hiatus, which was translating engineering technological verbiage in the Montreal *Herald* into everyday language for the reader.

The *Herald* was a racy tabloid specializing in crime news and sports; it's hard to imagine that it would have hired someone, even a freelancer, for technical translations. Another tall story?

Ivie's letter continues,

There is a disparity here in terms. By this time he had become to all and other purposes, a hermit. On the few occasions when he was seen in daylight ... he was always dressed in his bedroom gown and frequently roamed the hallways late at night in the same garb, in some instances creating fright to the odd late home-coming female.

He had a small apartment and slept on a low-slung camp chair and disallowed the janitors to enter at any time and on one occasion my youngest daughter, then a small girl, tried to follow him into his dwelling and was immediately shut out. However, she did say that his hallway was almost impassable as there were mountains of newspapers piled on either side right up to the ceiling. That this was true was demonstrated when the fire brigade came to clear out his place as a fire danger … and estimated there were eight tons of stuff to be cleared out.

Society ladies frequently left exotic fruits and other delicacies at his door which was found in a rotted condition and the firemen were surprised the floor had not given way. How he did his banking, his shopping, his everyday needs, the Good Lord only knows but we suspect he used the janitors.

There was one time when he called for one of the janitors to go at midnight to a certain place to bring back a small hand-held package triggering the suspicion that he was a dope addict. Well, we don't know but it wouldn't have been surprising. His garbage was carried outside in the middle of the night and dropped over the fence surrounding the garden of Trafalgar Girls' Private School. An oddball if ever there was one. He used to call my wife up on the phone and keep her on the line with endless desultory conversation.

As I said, he was well connected and at one time he loaned me a book and asked after I had read it to pass it along to Lady Allan. Make what you can of the foregoing.

I wrote back, asking Ivie if he could elaborate on some of these memories. I gave him a list of questions. Ivie wrote back that "this is almost like a student exam! Let me begin to tackle your 'exam' and see how I come out."

Question: Did Whitehead ever tell you about the Houdini incident?

An emphatic no. Oddly, though, he did talk much more freely with the children; occasionally he would intercept them as they passed the passage and tell them that he was unable to lie down to sleep and had a plate in his head. This he told to my elder pre-teen daughter at the time [Doreen] and her friends and they were always itching to get away from him as he seemed to want to talk a lot more than they were prepared to listen to. I have long been aware of the circumstances of Houdini's death ... but neither Smiley nor Price appear to have divulged very much at all as to what actually happened, such as the number of blows that were actually struck and if Whitehead did jump the gun before Houdini was ready.

Question: Were you aware of any links he might have had with spiritualists?

He did have a saturnine appearance which might have led some to associate him with the unworldly but nothing was ever heard to bear that out. You must remember that the 'Houdini' Whitehead and the man I knew must have been almost two diametrically opposed personages. On the other one hand you have the young buck with two young women chasing him around, and on the other the emaciated shadow of the man as I knew him.

Question: Can you elaborate on the plate in his skull?

This is an interesting point. I knew such a person who had a plate in his head and he was highly excitable to the stage where he would become almost hysterical and somewhat out of control. I would venture to suggest that the 'attack' came before the plate because Whithead was alleged to have dropped his studies after the plate was inserted.

Question: Can you say any more about the delicacies that were left at Whithead's door?

The feeling was that he was the recipient of good-willed patronage.

Which brings me to some of the more mundane facts of his existence—

Here was a man who was living without any visible means of support. I think we can safely assume that the engineering bit was merely a misinformative fallacy since he was no engineer. How he lived was a mystery. He was never seen in his street clothes except the times he was called for by car. I don't know anyone who ever saw any groceries being delivered, or anything else for that matter. Granted he was a night owl; to my knowledge there is no record of anyone arriving home late at night ever having heard the sound of a typewriter, or even during daylight hours.

He would not allow any of the janitors into his place and the curtains and windows had never been cleaned for years. My daughter says the package [delivered by the janitor] was from a drugstore which might sound significant but I don't recall any drugstore open until midnight in those days. The thought does occur to me that he might have been living on the pension he may have received from the power company resulting from the accident or the proceeds from a lump sum. … My wife remembers nothing particular except that he said he was a student in medicine and that when he would want to share or give away some of his goodies he always insisted that when he left them at her door she must not take them in until she heard the door of his apartment closing. How's that for secrecy?

My daughter says that his bathtub was filled with garbage, but I doubt that because I, myself, had seen him on several occasions around midnight crossing Guy Street in his gown, reach over the fence of the Trafalgar School for Girls and drop a small package there which I assumed would be like the size of the garbage he would accrue. Trafalgar at that time was situated halfway up Guy on the right-hand side just below Sherbrooke which would have been only a stone's throw away from Gordon's apartment.

Question: Can you say any more about returning the book to Lady Allan? (Lady Allen, the former Marguerite Ethel Mackenzie, was the wife of Sir Hugh Allan, owner of the Allan Shipping Line. They

Etta and Ivie Miller lived in the same downtown apartment
building as Whitehead.
"We were probably the only people in the building he had any
dealings with, other than the janitor,."
Photo by Don Bell

lived in a mansion on Upper Peel Street, known as Ravenscrag, now the Allan Memorial Institute.)

I am very sorry to say I am completely at a loss to remember the title of the book but I can assure you it was not a novel but a serious work. I did not know Lady Allan personally so sent the book on by mail with a note.

Question: Can you elaborate on the incident with the firemen in Whitehead's apartment?

What happened is that Gordon took sick and entered the hospital in which he died. The owners of the building then availed themselves of a long awaited opportunity to remove a very potential fire hazard in the course of which they called in the fire protection people who removed everything including, besides the papers, all sorts of things including many baskets of fruit which had accumulated over the years and been allowed to rot. We know nothing of who wound up whatever estate there was and the cause of his death was unknown to me.

When I met Ivie and Etta Miller in Montreal several months later, more was added to the haunting story. Ivie described what the "late home-coming ladies" would see when Whitehead wandered around the hallways in his gown.

"He was like an apparition, with his deep-set eyes, his dark hair and those thick eyebrows of his. I can tell you—they were scared!"

Etta, however, thought that he was "quite okay upstairs. Wasn't he?" she asked.

"But he had odd ways," she said. "We were probably the only people in the building he had any dealings with, other than the janitor, but for some reason he never dared set foot in the apartment. He would stand outside the door; he would hear the cat meowing inside. 'Do you have someone there?' he would utter. 'Ugh!' And after leaving something for us—a piece of cake or the vegetables that he hadn't touched—he would quickly return to his own apartment. It was as if he didn't want to be seen. Maybe because he wasn't dressed."

"He was never dressed," her husband remarked.

"But he wouldn't be in the nude?" Etta asked.

"No, but never in a suit."

Ivie remembered "a very good-looking young man with brown-coloured hair in a large two-seater sports car" who would pick Whitehead up sometimes.

"The thing that occurred to me, though it may be unfair and I'm not making any allegations, but I think there's a possibility," he conjectured, "that our friend may have been gay. But there was no proof about it. As far as I know he was never married."

Etta, however, professed that Whitehead "seemed to like the ladies."

"Unfortunately," Ivie Miller commented, "so many of the people are dead now who knew him, and the building itself of course is no longer there. One of the janitors who knew him fairly well—we had several during the twenty years we were in the building—was a man named Étienne. He was a kind of bum-boy for him, running his messages, but he's dead now. But he never set foot in the apartment. Nobody did."

The Millers' younger daughter Audrey, "who would have been seven or eight at the time," Etta said, "was asked once to run an errand for Whitehead, probably to pay the rent at the office. When she returned, she stood outside his door and thought she heard him say 'Come in, Audrey,' and she started to step inside, but he sternly told her to 'Stay there, Audrey.'"

His apartment was off limits, the Millers emphasized. Until the firemen came around, nobody had ever been seen going in or out. Not even the janitor had been inside.

"That time," Ivie remembered, "when the janitor was called up by Mr. Whitehead on the phone, at one in the morning, and asked to go to a certain restaurant on Ste. Catherine Street to pick up a small package, he left it in front of the door. He didn't go inside, he told us. What was in the package? He had no idea. So the question arises there: did Mr. Whitehead do drugs? We don't know. But it could quite conceivably be so. He looked like a man who did take drugs. Certainly he was a troubled individual."

Whitehead, Ivie and Etta agreed, never seemed to eat, never touched the baskets of figs and other treats which were left in front of his door. He looked sickly, undernourished.

"I wouldn't be surprised if that's what killed him. To look at the man, you wouldn't think he had the strength or the desire to hurt a fly. He wouldn't even know how to throw a punch," Ivie said, as he reminisced about this period more than twenty years after Houdini died.

That same evening I visited the Miller's widowed elder daughter, Doreen Turner. A community service worker in South Shore Brossard, she said she was around seven or eight when her family moved into the Grove Apartments in 1938 or 1939 and around twelve or thirteen when she started to know Whitehead, "or at least when he started to emerge from his apartment.

"I used to be afraid of him. He had a cadaverous look about him. His skin was a deathlike colour. His eyes were sunken. I never saw him in anything but a dressing gown and pyjamas or slippers, or an old horse blanket kind of thing.

"Sometimes he would get lonely and would come out of his apartment looking for someone to talk to. He would startle us. He never made any gestures or advances or anything. He just wanted to talk. He was an educated man, had a very nice diction; the conversations were usually in an intellectual vein. He seemed very well read. There were times when we tried to avoid him because he would talk and talk and talk."

Doreen couldn't remember many particulars about the conversations, although she recalled him telling her once about the steel plate in his head, saying that he had been a student at McGill when the accident occurred on a construction site up north. He suffered severe headaches because of it, he told her.

Did he talk about Houdini?

"Never, as far as I can remember."

She recalled the fire in the Montreal Repertory Theatre rehearsal studio next door although she was already married and gone by then. The theatre, founded by Sir Hugh and Lady Allan's daughter Martha, burned down on the night of March 5, 1952. The building was literally ripped apart by an enormous explosion.

"It was probably as a result of the fire, which caused rather heavy smoke and water damage in the building, that inspectors came around and saw what a hazard Whitehead's apartment was, that there was a risk the floor would cave in under the weight of the stacks of newspapers. I think it was condemned and he must have been given an ultimatum. Where he went after, I don't know. But I would imagine that a person like that who was forced to leave his premises would go further downhill. He certainly didn't look like a healthy man. He was very, very thin.

"My parents probably didn't tell you this, but after the fire department moved all his stuff out, the building became infested with cockroaches. It was as if they were disturbed and were scouting for new territory.

"It could be," she thought, "that his having been hit on the head at the construction site, which caused his skull to cave in, might have caused some brain damage. That would account for his odd behaviour. He did suffer a lot of pain and he did have those headaches. He was a recluse in the true sense of the word, a strange, mysterious person. I still get goose bumps thinking of him."

Her sister Audrey, reached in Arlington Heights, Illinois, said she was eight to ten years old when events with Whitehead took place in the building on Lincoln Avenue. As her mother had mentioned, she used to run errands for him. This went on for about one year.

"He was kind of isolated where his apartment was located. He had the hallway more or less to himself. He would send me to the grocery store on the corner of Guy for bread or milk, or to a small shop called Sam's which sold cigarettes and candies.

"Never once did he invite me in. The door was open six inches to a foot. I would just hand him the groceries through the opening. One time he left me standing by the door and went in to get the money to pay me. He always gave me a quarter for the errands, which was big money in those days. Although I was very timid, my curiosity got the better of me and I pushed the door open, just a little."

She saw his sanctum, the pathway like a wobbly footbridge through the piles of newspapers and magazines.

"I also have memories of moths. It seems that every time I ran an errand and returned with the groceries, a moth would fly out when he opened the door.

"He kept very much to himself. I don't remember him having any visits. When you saw him on the stairway, it was just a fluke. He didn't socialize. Just a little 'Hello', never more than that. He was tall and thin, gaunt-looking, and wore this hat with the brim turned down and a trench coat, belted, with the collar turned up. When he walked, he skulked. He didn't linger."

Unlike her sister, Audrey remembered him as "a man of very few words. I was afraid of him because of his demeanour. He had a kind of stern face with high cheek bones and an aquiline nose. I wasn't scared to the point of running away, but I knew my place with him."

Did she think he could have been ignited into violence?

"Well, there was never any noise or fights that I was aware of. But he was very withdrawn. Perhaps if his territory was invaded it might have annoyed him. He was very protective of his space and wouldn't let anyone get too close—for instance, just the way he opened the door when I ran his errands, keeping it ajar six inches and myself handing him the groceries through the opening. He was definitely weird. If the thing about Houdini is true, he might have been carrying this guilt with him."

26

The Price of Long Distance

~

I WAS DETERMINED to find Jacques Price—if he wasn't a figment of Sam Smiley's imagination. Nothing had been heard of him after the Whitehead blow, and he is mentioned only fleetingly in the later Houdini biographies. He was simply not thought to have had a prominent role in the tale; it was Smiley's story, after all, and Whitehead was the author of the fatal blow. Price just happened to be there.

But if he could be found, perhaps he'd have some memories of the incident, and could either back up Smiley's story or have his own. It was vital at least to find out if he really existed. There was no reason to doubt Smiley, whose version of the Houdini punch has been consistent over the years, but Price could lend credibility to what we knew.

Because Jacques Price hadn't graduated from McGill there was nothing much to go on other than an enrolment card on microfilm in the Registrar's office. Because of strict, and, one is tempted to add, archaic, university regulations, the office was reluctant to provide any information other than to confirm that a student named Jacques Price had been registered as a science undergraduate in the 1926-27 scholastic year and again in 1927-28. However, he dropped out in November 1927. His middle name was Isadore and he was born in Preston, England.

Perhaps Sam Smiley's memory could be jogged. It had been a couple of years since our last interview. Smiley was still sharp now, in 1984. "You're the fellow with the beard," he recalled when I phoned him. When I told him I was trying to trace Price and anything he could remember might help, he said he thought Price had returned home to England after he'd left McGill, but he'd lost touch with him. The only other clue he could offer was that Price might at one time have been a member of

Sigma Alpha Mu fraternity.

The Montreal chapter didn't have records going back further than fifteen years because fraternities had been banned on two occasions and the old membership files hadn't been kept. The chapter president suggested writing to headquarters in Carmel, Indiana. I wrote, and the letter came back with a typewritten message at the bottom of the sheet: "We do not show Mr. Price as ever being a member of Sigma Alpha Mu. Sorry."

And there it more or less stood for the period 1984 through 1990. Somewhere in that time I made some calls to England. I remember speaking to a Preston telephone operator, relating the Houdini punch story to her and asking her if she could suggest any old-timers in the Jewish community (his named "Isadore" suggested Jewish origin) whose memories might go back a distance. She suggested a man named Percy Goldberg—"He's an eighty-year-old who knows everybody." The only Price he knew was Ted, a bachelor who had died a few years earlier in his seventies. The age seemed to fit, but why would Jacques Price change his name to Ted? Probably no relation at all.

I asked Goldberg if he knew what Ted Price did for a living. "He was a clark," said the old man at the other end in a thick Midlands accent. "A clark?" Long pause, long-distance charges ringing up … eventually I understood that he was saying "clerk."

Percy Goldberg kindly offered to go to the Jewish cemetery and said if he found anything he'd ring back. It was bizarre to imagine that across the ocean deep in the English Midlands this octogenarian gentleman might rub dust off old stones, looking for the name of someone who may or may not have been in the dressing room in Montreal aeons ago when Harry Houdini had been walloped.

In the summer of 1990, I was living in Paris. I had a valise full of files, but hadn't written a word on Houdini. There was still that one missing piece in the puzzle: Price had to be found if Smiley's version of the dressing-room story was to stand up.

My son was studying at Oxford at the time, and it made good sense to combine a trip to see Daniel with a run up to Preston to see if any trace of Price could be found.

The first step was a visit to the British Cultural Centre on rue de Constantine in Paris to look through the Preston telephone directory. Some fifty J. Prices were listed, but no "J.I." I photocopied the names and jotted down the numbers of newspapers, synagogues, and cemeteries, not only in Preston but in larger Blackpool as well, eighteen miles from Preston. On the way out I asked one of the librarians if he had any suggestions about transportation to Preston. "Why in the world would anyone want to go to Preston?" he asked, dumbfounded. "It's one of the bleakest areas of England. It was a major linen centre years ago, but there's nothing there now of any touristic interest." He mentioned the Beatles' song about four thousand holes in the ground which he thought summed up Preston pretty well. (It's actually about Blackburn, only ten miles away.)

Long-distance calls continued for a few more days. I tried reaching the *Jewish Herald* in Manchester because if Price was Jewish they might have had a file on him, but it was out of business. Then the Preston *Citizen*. It had a charming address, Winckley Square, but it was a small weekly and they suggested trying instead the Lancashire *Evening Post*, a daily covering a much wider area. A reporter at the *Post* agreed to plant an article about the search, giving my Paris address in case any readers knew Price's whereabouts. "Please let us know if you have any replies," she said.

The caretaker at the Blackpool United Hebrew Congregation synagogue passed on the phone number of a "Reverend Braunold" who said he did know a Jackie Price, but had met him only once. He suggested trying a Mr. Goodstone or the president of the congregation, Mr. Cohen. Both confirmed that there was a Jackie Price in Manchester, but he would be much younger than the Price that was being sought. Cohen suggested trying Percy Goldberg, "who is eighty-nine and would know everybody from the old days." Could it be the same Percy Goldberg I'd left several years earlier rummaging through graves in the Preston cemetery? Of course it was.

He remembered our previous conversation. He talked again about Ted Price, repeating that he'd never married, had no children. But he had a sister, Anita, who might still be alive, but was no longer living in

Preston. He also passed on the name of another old-timer, Benjamin Spellman, who might have known Ted or Anita. He suggested phoning the office of the Preston cemetery, which had a Jewish section.

This all seemed a long way from the Houdini dressing room of 1926, but for some compelling reason I remained on the case.

"If you ever come to Preston," Percy Goldberg said, "look us up."

27

Izzy or Izzy Not?

~

BENJAMIN SPELLMAN did indeed know Teddy Price. They had met in the army in 1939. Price had died three or four years ago, and Spellman had been in charge of the funeral arrangements. He wasn't aware of Teddy having gone to Canada, but he had a brother, Isadore, who might have gone. "But wait," said Spellman, who was eighty years old and retired, "I'll speak to my wife. She's a historian of the Jewish community."

He called to her, "Did you know Teddy's brother?" "Yes," she said in the background. "He went to Canada."

The last time Spellman had seen the sister, Anita, was at Teddy's funeral. She was living in Barrow-in-Furness, he thought, but under her married name. He'd do some checking to try to locate her. "Phone me back in a week," he said.

I remembered that there was a shelf of Canadian phone directories, mostly old and falling apart, at the Centre culturel canadien, also on rue de Constantine. Wouldn't it be amazing if Price's name was in one of them? There was a promising listing in Toronto: J.I. Price. Certainly worth another long-distance call. A lady answered. Jessie Price she said her name was—"Sorry, I'm not the one you're looking for."

Perhaps Anita and other relatives of Teddy could be traced through cemetery records, just as Whitehead had been. A call to the Preston cemetery confirmed that there was a Teddy (Edward) Price buried there. He died September 19, 1978, age seventy-eight. The cemetery didn't have names of next-of-kin but suggested trying the funeral home.

I reached a woman with the marvellous name of Peggy Leatherbarrow at the Draper Funeral Home in Southport, a coastal resort eighteen miles from Preston. She made a cursory check of the files and couldn't find anything. But her sister, Jean Draper, who was away for a few days, would know where to look. Meanwhile, she suggested phoning Maureen Cohen, the secretary of the Southport Hebrew Congregation.

Maureen knew of Anita, whose married name, she said, was Langstrath. The Congregation had an address for her in Preston's Frenchwood district, but if she'd moved to Barrow-in-Furness it was probably an old address. Her phone number was unlisted. She suggested placing a call to a Mr. Lewis, who in turn referred to a Maurice Barker and his wife in Preston, who knew the Prices.

Yes, the Barkers confirmed, Teddy Price did have a brother, Izzy, who went to Canada. They thought he was dead, however. They didn't know how to reach Anita, but there was an older sister, Hilda, in Blackpool. They couldn't recall her married name. They didn't know where in Canada Izzy had gone, but they thought he was "in the engineering industry."

At the post office on Champs Élysée I found a Lancashire phone book which listed three Langstreths in Blackpool (spelled with an "e", not Langstrath, but Maureen Cohen could have been mistaken about the spelling), but none in Barrow-in-Furness. Optimism reigned.

I phoned Maureen Cohen again. She said she had tried to get Anita's number through her doctor "but she wouldn't give her phone number even to him." She suggested writing to Anita at the old Preston address which the synagogue had for her but she seemed to be a rather peculiar and eccentric person and Maureen's guess was that she wouldn't even answer. Maureen also suggested sending a letter to Maureen herself with all the details of the search, and in the meantime she would do everything to locate the other Price sister, Hilda.

No luck with the Langstreths in Blackpool. None were related to Anita. I also called the Southport Jewish Convalescent and Aged Home, thinking a Langstreth or a Price, since they were all well on in years, might be with them, but they had no one under either name.

I called a Canadian friend working for one of the British government information services in London, asking if there was any way he could obtain an unlisted number and if he thought there was a city directory for Barrow-in-Furness which might contain Anita's address. He phoned back to say that he'd found a D. Langstreth simply by calling the Barrow operator. If it wasn't the right party, he suggested planting a story in the *North West Evening Mail*, the Barrow-in-Furness newspaper, telling about the search for Anita.

Alas, the D. Langstreth lived with his sister, whose name was not Anita. But he said there were two other Langstreths in Markham, Lancashire, and found their numbers, and he said there was a Langstrath—with an "a"—Hotel in the Lakes District. As it turned out, the Markham Langstreths had no Anitas, and the original Langstraths from the Langstrath Hotel had long ago moved away.

Well aware that this Izzy Price I'd found out about might not even be the Houdini Price, I felt discouraged. Nevertheless, the next day, Sunday, July 22, 1990, I wrote to Maureen Cohen as she had suggested, summarizing the research. I also sent a lengthy letter to Anita Langstrath at the Preston address with a "Please forward" on the envelope, again summarizing the reasons for tracing her vanished brother. "It's been like looking for the proverbial needle in the haystack," I lamented. "I hope that you turn out to be the shiny needle and that your information will enable me to fill in the last shades and colours of the Houdini puzzle." I wasn't hopeful of getting a reply.

After mailing the letters, I phoned Benjamin Spellman again, as he'd asked me to do. He said there had been a memorial service over the weekend, and members of the Southport Congregation discussed the search, but nobody knew of Izzy Price or how to reach Anita or Hilda. He was sure Anita had moved to Barrow years ago, which meant that my long-worked-on four-page letter would probably never reached her. He suggested following through with calls to engineering associations in Canada.

Which is exactly what I did.

28

The Wrong Man?

~

THE TRIP TO PRESTON had to be put off. In mid-August 1990 I returned to Canada for a few weeks. Nguyen Van Hiep, an engineer friend of my son's, suggested trying to find Price through l'Ordre des Ingénieurs du Québec, which had its office on University Street in Montreal. The association had no Jack, Jacques, or Isadore Price in its records, but each Canadian province and territory has its own engineering association. The receptionist at l'Ordre patiently wrote down all the addresses and phone numbers.

Another flurry of calls followed.

"Hello, I'm phoning you from Quebec. I'm a journalist and I'm looking for a former engineer who may or may not have practised in your province. I was wondering if I gave you his name if you could run it through your computer."

There would be a quick scan through the records and—"Sorry." There was one brief rush of excitement when the Association of Professional Engineers of Nova Scotia came up with a Jacques Price, but he was born in 1912, not 1908. That would have made him fourteen years old when Houdini died. Also, he graduated from the University of Toronto in 1939. It wasn't likely he was at McGill thirteen years previously.

But I tried anyway. The address was a Halifax post office box. Nova Scotia telephone information had a number for him. I called, and a gentleman who seemed well on in years answered. I asked if he was Mr. Price, and he said yes. I introduced myself and came right to the point.

"I wonder, Mr. Price, if by any chance you are the Jacques Price from Preston, England who once studied at McGill and was in the dressing room when Harry Houdini, in 1926, received a punch to the midsection that later caused his death."

"No, I'm afraid you have the wrong man."

"You weren't born in Preston, England?"

"Afraid not."

"Well, thanks anyway. Sorry to have bothered you."

"No trouble."

For some reason, at the time it didn't strike me as anything more than a coincidence that there could be two engineers in Canada with the same last name, and the same rare (for English-speaking persons) first name, Jacques.

But the retired engineer Jacques Price in Halifax, at least in his few words spoken on the phone, didn't appear to have any trace of English accent—not that he would have.

So it was obviously the wrong man. Or so I thought.

Rather than pursue it further, I took the advice of the friend in London and wrote the editor-in-chief of the paper in Barrow-in-Furness, the English submarine capital, asking for help. I suspected the letter would go into the crackpot or crank file and be thoroughly ignored.

It was time to start thinking seriously again about nipping up to Preston and knocking on doors. Anita hadn't answered the letter, which probably never reached her. And there wasn't any news from Maureen Cohen about Hilda.

In mid-September I flew back to Paris and after kissing my wife hello, bought a five-day round-trip train-and-ferry ticket for London, whence it would be a few hours to Preston.

29

Presto! — Preston

A COUPLE OF INTERCITY trains from London and presto!, "Proud Preston", as the Borough Council Official Guide describes the late great linen capital of the British Isles, halfway up to Scotland. It is said that the temperance movement started here in 1834.

The sky is darkening. It's pissing buckets. The streets are empty. The bed-and-breakfasts on Fishergate, the main street, are one after another full. Finally, a dismal place off Fishergate run by a new-age religious cult has a room; the incense is hardly strong enough to stanch the foul odours being secreted by the moist walls, the musty blankets, the warped furniture, and probably the holes in the ground. Indeed, as the librarian at the British Cultural Centre in Paris had asked, why would anyone in their right mind want to visit Preston?

But it's in such obscure settings that the most amazing unexpected things can happen.

The morning was just as drenchy. I packed up my bag and called a Red Rose cab. But as soon as I stepped inside the vehicle and heard a friendly "Where yer goin' to, mate?", the clouds, overhead and in the mind, seemed to clear up.

His name was Harry Napier. A chatty bloke he was.

"Are yer on horliday, are yer?" he asked.

I briefly told him about the Houdini punch. You never know who knows what. He lit up. He had been to Canada himself a few years ago, he said, had a cousin there, a ju-jitsu instructor with the RCMP in Montreal, now retired, living in Vancouver. He'd visited him in Montreal ten years ago. "That where yer from, mate? Montreal?"

I asked him if he knew the Prices. Price is a common name, he said. Which one? Jacques?, I asked. No. Teddy? No. Then what about

Langstreth? Did he know any Langstreths in the Preston area?

"Langstrath? Yar. Richard Langstrath. Spelt with an 'a'. Not Lang-streth. Used to live on Wellington Street. Had a block of flats there which he sold. I wuz livin on Wellington Street meself near his block till I got meself married twenty-one yers ago. Tall bloke he was, he'd be in his sivinties now if he's still alive. Last time I saw him wuz on the street three or four years ago. His wife? Can't recall her name. She wuz kinda peculyer. She had vision problem. Wore thick spectacles. She had to be able to see yer close up or rec'nize yer voice before she could socialize with yer."

Could this be Anita's husband? The first spelling given by Maureen Cohen was "Langstrath". I asked him to continue to the Frenchwood address, but if it wasn't the right party we would drive back to Wellington and start ringing doorbells to see if any of the tenants knew Richard Langstrath, the former owner of the blocks.

"What about your own name?" I asked Harry out of curiosity. "Napier isn't very English. It sounds French. We used to have a hockey player in Montreal called Mark Napier."

"Yar. My father always claimed we wuz descended from Count Napier."

"Count Napier? Who was he?"

"Awvn't gawt a clue."

We arrived at the Frenchwood address. It was a semi-attached rose-brick bungalow on a street courting the Ribble River.

Harry waited in front. There were two small cars parked on the driveway. I walked to the arched doorway and rang the bell but didn't hear it ring. It seemed jammed, maybe broken. I knocked a couple of times. No one came. The curtains were drawn. There weren't any lights on. Then I tried the neighbour on the right, across the driveway. No answer there either. Then the left, which was the other half of the semi-detached house. A woman came to the door but didn't open. I pressed my lips to the glass-frame upper portion, and asked if her neighbours were the Langstraths. I faintly heard her reply that they were. Are they an old couple? Yes. She signalled that I should try around the back, which I did. I knocked again, and called out "Journalist!", as one would call

"Police!" This time she opened the door. She said there were a lot of attacks in the neighbourhood which was why she didn't open before. She wasn't on very friendly terms with her neighbours, the woman was peculiar, there was some friction between them, she didn't want to get into it. Yes, she did think the woman was called Anita but wasn't sure. If the cars are parked in the driveway, it means they are probably there, she said. They're usually not up and about in the morning. "You should come back after lunch, or in the evening."

Well, at least I was on the right track. If Anita Langstrath was living here in the Frenchwood district of Preston, the obvious deduction, dear Watson, was that the Barrow-in-Furness address was a false lead. But why didn't anyone answer? The cars were parked in front. Perhaps they peaked through the curtains and saw this confused American-looking person and assumed it was the Houdini researcher and didn't want anything to do with bloke showing up just like that, uninvited on their doorstep.

I told Harry Napier to drive me back to Wellington Street for the second plan of action. I could return to Frenchwood in the afternoon and knock a little harder. On the way, he pointed out St. Walburge's Roman Catholic Church. "It's a Preston landmark, got the third tallest spire in Britain," Harry informed me. The fact that it was designed by Hansom, the same bloke who "invented" the Hansom cab, probably gave it special appeal to my Hansom man Harry Houdini Napier.

We drove up to the rundown-looking flats on Wellington and I started ringing the bells at number 79, 81, and 83, which were the flats Napier thought that Langstrath had at one time owned. Maybe there'd be at least one old-timer who remembered him. But no one responded.

Count Napier drove us back to the B & B. I didn't contemplate staying another night in that dismal house, haunted by gurus and kooks, so Napier drove us to the train station. I put my valise in a locker and phoned Maureen Cohen. She apologized for not answering the letter, although it was hard to make out what she was saying through the train announcements: "Plaitform four … train now ready to depart from Plaitform four … Intercity service to London, Plaitform four." I asked her if she had the phone number of Anita's doctor, Dr. Nelson. Even though Anita wouldn't give her phone number even to him, perhaps the doctor had an address for her. She found the number but advised it would be a waste of time to try to phone him today. "He won't answer because it's *yontiff* and he'll be in *shul*, but you can call him Sunday."

Perhaps, I suggested, if Anita and her husband didn't answer the door (if Frenchwood was in fact where they lived), it was because they were observing the holiday. Not likely, Maureen said: Anita's husband wasn't Jewish and she wasn't in the least religious. If you're in Southport, Maureen invited, you should drop by at the *shul*.

But instead, in the afternoon I returned to the bungalow facing the Ribble River and rang the bell. A tall man, probably in his seventies, with white hair, a furrowed brow, his glasses horn-rimmed on top, came to the door. After I explained the reason for the visit, without any hesitation he invited me in. He said he didn't have too much time. The house was in disarray. Dick Langstrath, for this was who the gentleman was, explained that he he'd brought his wife—Anita—to the hospital yesterday with pneumonia and other complaints and he was just on his way there. It had been a real rough couple of days, he said, but it was lucky I'd come today rather than yesterday, "otherwise she would have been here and you wouldn't have got your foot in through the front door." Yes, she received the letter, he said. "I started to write to you, but she didn't want me to and besides my hands shake so I decided to give up. She said you'd probably make a lot of money out of the book. I told her he'd put her picture in it, but she still didn't want to have anything to do with it.

"But I'm glad you came by," he said. "If you journeyed all this way the least I can do now is help you as much as I can. Did you come by this morning? I thought I heard the doorbell ringing but I got in late last night after leaving her at the hospital. I haven't been able to sleep for weeks because she's been so ill and I've been taking care of her. Last night I drank half a bottle of scotch and fell asleep on the armchair in the living room. I have to go to the hospital soon. You can come with me. But we still have a few minutes."

What about her brother Jack, or Jacques, I asked. Had he ever met him?

"Yes, this exactly what I would have written if she'd let me," Langstrath said. "She had a brother Jack who lived in Canada. But he died three or four years ago. He left Preston around age sixteen. He went to McGill, he was a civil engineer and a squadron leader within the Canadian air force during the Second War. He designed airfields I believe. After the war he married a Canadian girl and they lived in Nova Scotia. The family lost touch with him for twenty-odd years, but then Jack's mother received a letter from the University of Toronto because he'd been awarded the King's Medal for his service during the war. The family traced him through the university to Nova Scotia. He wrote to the family in 1965 and he said he'd come on a visit but he was always very busy. He finally came for a few days in 1966 and I drove him and his brother Teddy around. He had his own company. He was a consulting engineer and he built waterways in Canada."   Did Langstrath know anything about the Houdini blow? No, and, to his knowledge the family had not been aware of this episode in his brother-in-law's past either. In fact, the first time he heard about it was in my letter. Nor did he think that Price mentioned it to his brother and sisters when he visited Preston in 1966 to be reunited with them. The subject of Houdini as far as he knew never came up.

Langstrath was soon rummaging through his wife's effects, looking for letters Jack had written. "She'd be mad as hell if she knew I was going through her purse. She'd be down my throat." But he thought there was no harm done if he went through it and found something helpful especially since I'd come all this way. "We've been together forty-odd years. She's dynamite. She's Jewish, you know. She has arthritis and she's lost her sight in one eye. Cataracts." He found a letter, read it aloud, too fast to jot down more than a few phrases, but essentially Jack Price was thanking them "for the great pleasure you gave me during the two days at home" and asking the family's forgiveness "for having neglected you all over the years."

Did Jack have children? Yes, he had a daughter, he thought, named Karen who was living in Nova Scotia—but he didn't have an address for her. But there was an address on the envelope of Price's letter, a box number in Windsor, Nova Scotia. Windsor was small. It was curious, I was thinking, that he'd lived in Nova Scotia, as did the Jacques Price traced through the engineering association who said he was not the Houdini Jacques Price. Now at least I probably had the right one. Even though he presumably died a few years ago, his wife, if she were still alive, and his daughter probably could be tracked down with some phone calls. From one of the letters, it was established that his wife's name was Margo. Did Anita have any photos of her brother, I asked?

Langstrath disappeared and came back a moment later with a matted eight-by-ten-inch black-and-white photo of his brother-in-law, which he said had been found amongst Teddy Price's effects after he'd died, in a tin box that also contained Teddy's prayer book. The photo showed a handsome-looking man in his thirties, with strong features and a resolute expression. He was attired in an RCAF uniform with burnished buttons and a winged decoration on the forepart of the cap.

Langstrath wanted to get to the hospital before the visiting hours ended. I could wait for him in the lobby, he said. In the car he mentioned that Anita had a sister. Hilda Baker was her married name. She lived in Blackpool, twenty-two miles from Preston. She was older than his wife, in her eighties, but last time he saw her which admittedly was a few years ago, she was lucid. She could probably provide more details about her brother Jack.

When Langstrath came out from Anita's room, he was distraught. Anita had tubes down her throat and wasn't in very good shape.

When we returned to his car in the parking lot, I told him I'd be interested in meeting Hilda and asked if he knew which would be the best way to get to Blackpool. "Let me think about that," he said. He stopped for some petrol. "If you phone," he said, "it will surprise her and she'll be confused. It's better just to show up at the door." He said he'd drive me. He hadn't seen her in a few years. Hilda wasn't on good terms with Anita but as far as he knew she had nothing against him.

On the road to Blackpool, zipping along on the left side in the wee Fiat, like an insect among the mammoth lorries, Langstrath started to relax. He remembered Price's visit in 1966.

"He had hired a car and I drove him and his brother Teddy around the countryside for two days. I was the outsider in a sense. They had a

Dick Langstrath, 1991, holding a photograph of Jacques Price.
Photo by Don Bell.

lot to say to each other. They hadn't seen each other since childhood, since Jack left for Canada. He struck me as being a quiet fellow, like Teddy, whom I always admired. He was poised, not boastful, even though he was quite rich, I think."

When we reached Bispham on the outskirts of Blackpool, he had trouble finding Hilda's house. She'd moved from the old address Langstrath remembered. The woman who lived in the house suggested we try some of the neighbours who might know where Hilda lived. They in turn suggested trying the newsagent at the corner. The newsagent, who was also the postmaster, suggested trying Number 202 on such-and-such a street, which we did and just as we arrived at the address (Langstrath was thoroughly enjoying this detective work; it was taking his mind off Anita's illness), a car pulled up and a man and his wife stepped out, the man was suspicious at first because he'd caught us on his lawn peeking through the windows like a couple of voyeurs. After some explanations, he said they were the Bakers but not the same Bakers being sought, who were at Number 208 just a few doors away. Nobody came when we rang and knocked. There was no sign of life inside, but just as we were about to leave Langstrath spotted a woman crossing the street, a small boy clutching her hand, and recognized Hilda with her grandson David.

A gentle-looking white-haired lady, she seemed surprised but also pleased to see Langstrath and invited us in for scones and tea. There was much to talk about—the family, Anita's health, and the misunderstandings that had occurred in the past—but as far as the story of Jack Price and Houdini was concerned, Hilda had never heard it before. Yes, she confirmed, her brother had died a few years ago. He had a married daughter, Karen Virginia. She corroborated the information that Langstrath had given, that he'd been a squadron leader with the RCAF during the war and had been a consultant engineer for the government in Canada, building roads and waterways. Just as we started to talk about Price, Hilda's son Malcolm and his wife came in; there were further reconciliations and discussions, Langstrath explaining that, yes, Anita could be difficult at times but either she liked someone or she didn't and that's just the way she was which is what he learned being married to her for forty years. Hilda refilled the kettle and scones were offered again, passed around by the grandson, as family problems were sorted out.

Hilda didn't know where Price's daughter had settled. She was married to a barrister, she thought, and they might be living in Ireland because his family was from there and they'd gone there on their honeymoon. Yes, she had a picture of Jack when he was around eighteen, "but you wouldn't want that." Yes, I would, please; that was just around the time he was in Montreal. But she didn't have it in the house. Her daughter Lynn had it and she was away on holiday. When Lynn came back, she'd ask her for the photos and cuttings about her brother Jack or Jacques Price and she would duplicate the photo and make copies of the clippings and send them to me. I had the feeling, and so did Langstrath apparently, that at first Hilda might have suspected I was a detective, hired to be a witness to a debate about family heirlooms. Unfortunately it would have been too obstrusive to have turned on the tape recorder to capture this Pinteresque dialogue with its nuances and pauses as the conversation shifted from one side of the room to the other.

Later, in the car Langstrath suggested writing to Hilda to remind her what I'd come for. He thought she was too overwhelmed by the visit to have had time to think clearly about her late brother or provide more information. Driving along the roadway in the pitch black Midlands night, he said he regretted never having asked Jack about the Houdini incident. "I'm sure if I'd asked him, he would have told me."

We stopped at the Preston General Hospital and I waited in the lobby while Langstrath visited his wife. When he came down he was relieved. Her condition had improved. It was getting late now. There was a night train to London, but I decided not to take it. He dropped me off at the Railway Hotel Pub where I had a bag of peanuts and a Matthew Arnold: this definitely wasn't the soberside part of town, not where temperance movement founder Joseph Livesay and the teetotallers would have felt comfortable. With a few phone calls I found a room in a hotel a few bus-stops away on Grimshaw Street.

After settling in, I went down to the bar to soak up the ambiance and size up the day's findings. The regulars looked like they dropped in for a pint or two after an evening of soccer rioting. It was hard to tell if they were honest-to-goodness hooligans or just workers from British Aerospace, Preston's largest company.

The hotel owner was working at the bar. He came over and asked the usual question about yer being on holiday in Preston? You never know who can tell you about what, so I filled him in on the project. Yes, he knew of Houdini, he said, but what really fascinated him was the way he died. He gave the usual version: the dressing room, the student who was an amateur boxer, the punch ... but with one difference. He said the author of the blow was named Barrett. He remembered the name because his own name was Barrett. I informed him, gently, because it wasn't the sort of bar where you'd like to start an argument, that the name of the student wasn't Barrett, but Whitehead. He then mentioned thatHoudini had once performed in Preston.

I would later check and found that Houdini had played the Hippodrome Theatre in Preston in 1906. As he wrote in his diary, he faced one of his most difficult challenges there. As he usually did when he arrived in a new town, to publicize his show he went straight to the local jail and asked the guards to strip him, search him, put him in prison garb, handcuff him, lock him up, and throw away the keys. Usually he would be out within minutes, but Preston jail had unorthodox handcuff and cell locks which almost defeated him. He injured his hand trying to escape, grappled with the locks for three hours before finally freeing himself. Houdini told his jailers, "Your prison is one of the most secure places I have ever come across."

Price's parents undoubtedly knew of Houdini's prison exploits. Perhaps they were in the audience at the Hippodrome. It seemed safe to assume that Price grew up hearing stories of Houdini's stunts and gladly accompanied Smiley to meet the magician at the Princess Theatre.

30

A Letter from Hilda

~

Don,

As promised I am writing to you regarding my late brother 'Jack', Consultant Civil engineer in Canada.

The following may help you a little but until my daughter is back from America I'm sorry I cannot send you the cuttings & photograph which she has.

Perhaps you already know he was a Squadron Leader in the Royal Canadian Air Force & and he was married to Margo Reece.

After coming out of the Air Force he held a high position in the Town planning, giving estimates etc. for water & railways, he was mentioned in dispatches for planning an Airfield & my elder brother who sadly died approx. six years ago used to visit the library & always found his name listed under his profession, he also had a degree in London England & it was only when his name did not appear that we knew he had died.

His daughter Karen Virginia will be 45 years old now & the last time I saw Jack was when she got married 24 years ago, and she spent her honeymoon in Ireland. I think she was a nurse before she married, although, I believe he was in London every year he was always too busy to visit his family.

We completely lost touch when he got married & for my mother's sake I felt I had to find him & I did manage to trace him through the Air Force & we kept in touch again for a while but we lost touch again.

You should have little or no trouble in tracing him as he was very well known all over Canada especially in Toronto where he qualified.

For the time being this is all I can think of so I must wish you luck in your findings & shall be interested to hear of your progress.

Best Wishes
Sincerely
Hilda Baker (Mrs.)

P.S. He was the chief Consulting Officer in the Town Planning Office, as you will note when I am able to send you the newspaper cuttings, prior to taking up office on his own in Windsor, Nova Scotia as a Consultant.

31

Yours Slickly, Sam

"AND AWAY WE WENT at a slapping pace," says the Squire in one of Thomas Chandler Haliburton's *Sam Slick the Clockmaker* tales.

Windsor, a community of 4,000, forty-five miles from Halifax across the Avon River Causeway—gateway to the Annapolis Valley—is the birthplace of Haliburton, the nineteenth-century judge and author recognized as Canada's first, and some say best, humourist, predating Stephen Leacock by seventy years. His opinionated, gossipy Sam Slick creation is still widely quoted in "these 'em parts" and although Slickville could be anywhere in the Atlantic provinces or New England ("Yankee country"), Windsor, his home, was most certainly on Haliburton's mind when he had his quaint clockmaker deliver such slick lines as "They do nothin' in these parts but eat, drink, smoke, sleep, ride about, lounge at taverns, make speeches at temperance meetin's and talk about 'House of Assembly.'"

When I was back in Quebec, it took only a few calls to find someone who knew of Jacques Price. It was, in fact, Jack Price who knew of Jack Price. The number of the first, in Hantsport, a few miles from Windsor, was provided by Nova Scotia telephone information when I asked for Jack or Jacques Price, thinking his widow, if she was alive, might have kept the number under his name. Jack Price in Hantsport said he wasn't the one I wanted, but he used to know by sight a Jack Price from Windsor who worked at one time as a town engineer. He suggested calling the Windsor Town Office.

A clerk there said she didn't recognize the name, but she was relatively new and would make some inquiries. A moment later she returned to the phone and confirmed that Price had worked for the town at one time. She also confirmed that Karen was this Jack Price's daughter's name. She amiably provided the names and phone numbers of several people who could help in the search, including the deputy mayor who had been Windsor's fire chief for fifty years.

But eventually it was a historian and biographer, Katherine Anslow, who provided the leads. She'd known Jack Price and his wife socially through bridge, she said. They were both avid players. They'd come to Windsor for his work and left ten or fifteen years ago after he'd retired, and settled in Halifax. She had never heard of the Houdini incident, but, she said, Price was an odd character.

"He just wasn't one of the gang, if you know what I mean. They were … a little different from everybody else." One of the bridge group, a doctor, knew them better than she did. She'd try to reach him and suggested I phone back later.

From the doctor Katherine Anslow obtained the address and phone number of the Price's house in Halifax, and found out that their daughter Karen had been married to a lawyer and was divorced and her married name, which she still used, was Mann. It might be possible to trace her through telephone directory assistance. She said her bridge companions had recently visited them in Halifax. By "them" I presumed she meant Price's wife and daughter, since Price himself, according to the Preston relatives, was deceased.

I decided to try to find the wife and daughter, but something else was on my mind. I was thinking about the phone call I had made six years earlier to the Jacques Price in Halifax, the wrong man, who politely, adamantly denied being a witness to the punch. I checked through the telephone statements in my back tax files, and sure enough, the phone number was the same. It was obviously the same man, who meantime had apparently passed away.

But it made no sense. I was befuddled, feeling *wamblecroft*, to use the colourful Sam Slick term for confusion. There was discrepancy in the birth dates, and if this was the same person, why would he have denied it?

The mystery deepened when I phoned the University of Toronto archives, which found a clipping on Jacques Price who graduated from the Faculty of Applied Sciences and Engineering *in 1958*. The clipping was from Windsor's *Hants Journal*. This Price had given a speech at one of the technical sessions of the American Water Works Association Conference at White Point Beach, Nova Scotia on automation in water systems. The article identified him consulting civil engineer and a member of various professional associations, and said he'd held the rank of Squadron Leader in the Works & Building Branch of the RCAF during the Second War and was mentioned in Despatches in the King's Honours.

Could any more information be pried out of McGill's fortress-strong Registrar's Office? After I explained the mission to an administrator in the office, his card was pulled out again. It was reconfirmed that Jacques Isadore Price, born in Preston in 1908, was enrolled in 1926. Could he have fibbed about his age to get into McGill? Not likely, the administrator said. He would have needed a high school certificate or equivalent. Two tidbits were offered: "It looks like he dropped out because he was ill at some point. 'Ill during … something or other'. And there is something on his card which he crossed out about his parents being Jewish." Had it occurred to Price to delete references to religion to improve his chance to be accepted by McGill? As Sam Slick asked himself, "Do you jist pretend to … make believe as if you were a-goin' the whole hog in it? Ax me no questions and I'll tell you no lies."

I still wanted to ax a few questions.

32

Phil and Roz and Karen

THROUGH TELEPHONE DIRECTORY assistance in Halifax I got numbers for a lawyer named David Mann and a Dr. K. Mann. It so happens that my cousin there, Dr. Philip Belitsky, was a professor of Urology at Dalhousie University. His wife Roz is a physiotherapist. If Karen Mann was a doctor, they might know her.

"Of course we know her," said Roz. "She lives just a few doors away. She isn't a medical doctor but has a Ph.D. She's working part-time at two jobs, one involving blood work and another in hospital administration. She's a very nice lady, from an old Halifax family. She's divorced and has three children."

I told Roz about the Houdini research. She'd never heard the story from Karen, whom she'd known for seventeen or eighteen years. She was surprised Karen might be half-Jewish.

It was incredible that Jacques Price's daughter could be living a few houses away from a first cousin. Perhaps in his magical way, this is how Houdini willed it to be.

Karen answered on the first ring. "This is one of those 'It's a small world' calls," I started. She seemed like a friendly enough person, as Roz said she would be. I explained I was phoning from Quebec and was a cousin of her neighbours. I described my research and asked if she was the daughter of Jacques and Margo Price, which she confirmed. She was quite amazed when I recounted how I'd traced her through the family in Preston. Yes, Hilda Baker and Anita Langstrath were her aunts. Then came a stunning revelation.

"My father is still alive."

"What? They told me in Preston he died years ago."

THE MAN WHO KILLED HOUDINI

"He's very much alive, and he lives in Halifax."

"And your mother?"

"My mother as well."

"And is he in good health?"

"Yes. He's just a bit hard of hearing."

"And the Houdini incident?"

"He never mentioned it to me. But I should explain that he's a very private person. When did the incident take place?"

"In 1926."

"My father went to the University of Toronto. I'm not sure if he went to McGill. In 1926 he would have been only fourteen years old."

"Not if he was born in 1908."

"But he was born in 1912."

"But the McGill Registrar's Office lists the Jacques Price from Preston as being born in 1908."

"My mother always told me that she and my dad were the same age. She was born in 1912."

"Are you sure he never told you about the Houdini punch?"

"Absolutely sure. It's the first I've heard about it."

"And your mother?"

"She never mentioned it."

"Since your father is hard of hearing," I proposed, "it might be difficult for him to talk to me on the phone. I wonder if you could ask him about it?"

"How soon would you have to know?"

"As soon as possible." I explained that I'd be willing to leave for Halifax if her father would discuss the incident.

"I won't be able to do anything tonight, but I'll speak to him tomorrow."

After hanging up, I had that vertiginous feeling of *wamblecroft* again. A Jacques Price had been found, but perhaps he was nowhere near McGill in 1926 and was not the same Jacques Price who was in Houdini's dressing room.

Karen described him as a private person. Kay Anslow said he was a character. Was it because there was a mystery in his past? Did this have

to do with Houdini? A falsified birth date? A birth religion he preferred
to deny?

I waited a couple of days but Karen didn't phone back. On November
7, since I was planning to leave soon for the winter, I phoned her.

As during the first call, she was charming and friendly, but there
was a note of prudence in her voice. Yes, she had spoken to her father,
and there was something to do with Houdini, "but you have to understand, as I told you the other day, my father is a very private person and
he just doesn't want to get involved. He doesn't talk very much about his
past. It's something that happened a long time ago and he would prefer
not to talk about it. He was in Montreal, but he wouldn't confirm [being
in the dressing room] or not confirm it."

She inferred it would be an invasion of his privacy to proceed any
further. She said she appreciated all my efforts and the work that had
gone into trying to trace her father, "but it's his life, and I guess it's up to
him whether or not he'd like to talk about it, but he'd prefer not to."

I explained that there would be nothing negative about her father
in the book. It was just to get his version of the incident. To the contrary,
I assured her, according to Smiley it was her father who had the presence
of mind to pull Whitehead off Houdini, so if anything he was really the
hero of the story. She said she understood, but she didn't think it would
do any good to explain this to him again. He seemed resolved.

"If I wrote to him?"

"Yes, you could do that."

"If I phoned him?"

"It's not likely," Karen said, "that he will discuss it."

Once again I mentioned the family in Preston who thought her
father was deceased. "He hasn't been in communication with the family,"
she pointed out, but it was a private family matter. I told her that Hilda
wanted me to convey a message to Karen's mother, if I found her, that
Margo should get in touch with her and that I should pass on Hilda's
address.

"If I just showed up at the door, do you think your father would
speak to me?" I asked.

"I don't think he would appreciate that."

There it stood for two days. Phil and Roz were in Montreal for a conference that weekend. I phone Roz at the hotel and recounted the two conversations. Roz thought it might be a good idea if I did just show up at the door. "It's so much easier to dismiss someone on the phone." Roz said she always thought the family was pure Halifax church-going Protestant. Perhaps Karen didn't even know she was part Jewish. She'd never met her father but had once met Karen's mother at a tea or a women's social function. "She struck me as being very forthright, like Karen, a very fine lovely lady." She thought it was rather odd that Price, if he had been in the dressing room, did not want to discuss it. "Usually people at that age like to talk about the past in a bravado sense. Anyway, if you do show up you can stay with us."

33

For God's Sake, Stop!

WHAT IF PRICE SLAMMED the door in my face? It was mid-November, not the best of seasons for visiting the Atlantic coast. Plus I was already booked to return to France in a few days. I decided that rather than play paparazzi and show up by surprise on his doorstep, I would phone so I could at least find out if he'd talk at all. If he was receptive, with luck he'd still be around in the spring and then I'd be able to combine a visit to the cousins and some touristic wandering through the Maritimes with a visit to the Houdini witness. There didn't seem to be any harm in sounding him out on the phone.

On the morning of November 14, 1990 I dialed the Halifax number. A woman answered, probably Mrs. Price. I asked if Mr. Price was home. She said, "One moment please." He came to the phone. "Hello"—in a soft, gentle voice. I stumbled through a recitation about this possibly being a rather delicate subject, but I was writing a book about Harry Houdini and I understood that he was the Jacques Price who was a friend of Sam Smiley and was in the room at the Princess Theatre when White-head had tested Houdini with a blow to his stomach.

There was a long pause, but he didn't hang up and so far had not reacted with shock or anger. He said, abruptly, that he couldn't talk about that now because he had company. He suggested phoning him back. When would be a good time? Tomorrow, around noon, he said.

I had to be in Montreal the next day since the flight for Paris was to leave the day after. I wondered if it was a brush-off and if he'd conveniently be absent when I phoned. But he did reply. Immediately afterwards, I wrote down everything I could remember of the conversation.

I introduced myself and again started to describe the Houdini research. But he broke in. "What did you say your name was?" I had forgotten about his hearing and was speaking too rapidly. The clatter of traffic outside the window of my B & B probably made it harder for him to hear.

I pronounced my name slowly and clearly. Then he said, "I cannot understand why you are conducting this vindictive investigation which is causing my family and myself so much anguish."

It felt like someone had pounded me on the head with a jackhammer. I was caught off-guard.

"But Mr. Price," I finally protested, "I have not been investigating *you*. I've been trying to trace you because it's very important to try to find out, for the sake of the biography on Houdini, as much as possible about the events leading up to his death."

Price asked what I did for a living. I told him "author" and added "journalist", knowing how the latter often evokes negative reactions. I tried to answer all his questions, especially about credentials: *Weekend* magazine, the CBC, the Montreal *Gazette*, books written.

"What publication are you writing this for?" he asked.

I told him truthfully that I didn't know; when the book was closer to completion I would go the rounds to find a publisher. I really didn't mean to cause him any anguish, but was curious to hear his version of the dressing-room incident. There was absolutely nothing negative that would be written about him. To the contrary, since, according to Smiley, he had pulled Whitehead off Houdini.

He asked if I had read any books about Houdini, then referred to Milbourne Christopher's work. "Everything about the incident is explained there."

I told him that Christopher and the other Houdini biographers who mention the incident (he seemed surprised to hear there were others) had as their source Sam Smiley, but it would be interesting to hear his version.

He hadn't hung up, and in a weird way seemed to be warming up. I decided to be bold and ask him some specific questions about the atmosphere in the dressing room. Did he remember, for instance, the title of the book that Whitehead, according to Smiley, had borrowed from Houdini and was returning?

"No, I can't. It was all so long ago. I don't even remember what I was doing there. We were in the dressing room for a short time with Houdini. It was in the afternoon. But we didn't even see his show."

"Do you remember anything about Whitehead?"

"I remember he was a rather tall fellow. That's about all that I can recall."

"Do you remember how he punched Houdini?"

"Houdini was on the couch, going through his mail I think. I don't remember why Whitehead came in or what he was doing there."

"Do you think he knew Houdini?"

"I wouldn't know. You're asking me questions—it was all so long ago. Sixty-four years. Houdini was flat on his back. Houdini forced his stomach muscles, structuring himself in such a way to withstand the blow. I don't know who Whitehead was. I'd never seen him before and never saw him again after that. I don't know why he came in or what he was doing there."

Could he remember anything about Whitehead's attitude? Did he seem angry or aggressive?

"I would be guessing."

"There's a theory," I plunged in, "that Whitehead may have deliberately wanted to hurt Houdini, that he may have been acting on behalf of the spiritualists whom Houdini had been so fervently exposing. Do you think that's possible?"

"It's the first time I've heard that theory. It's purely hypothetical. I wouldn't know."

"Can you recall," I asked, "if Whitehead punched Houdini only once, to test him, or did he keep hitting him?"

"All I can remember is that I cried out words to the effect of 'For God's sake, stop!'"

" 'For God's sake, stop!?' "

"Yes. They may not have been my exact words, but words to that effect."

"Smiley said that he struck Houdini several times, that it was a flurry of blows."

"I don't remember how many times he hit him. It was more than once. There were several blows. As I told you, it was so long ago, I really can't tell you much more."

I should have asked other questions, but I was so amazed to have found Price, alive, and to have him confirm that he was in Houdini's dressing room, that the little that he did remember and offer was pure manna.

Price went on to talk about the Nova Scotia winter and living by the sea. "Do you sail?" he asked. He said he had a lot of things to keep him busy. He still had a drop of English accent. I asked him his age.

"I'm getting on," he offered.

"Could we meet in the spring?" I asked, so I could photograph him and tape his story.

"If I'm still around," he replied. "You better write or phone first."

We had spoken for about forty-five minutes, half of it friendly chitchat after we'd covered the Houdini essentials. I gave him both my Sutton and Paris address in case he could think of anything else. He said if anything came to mind, he would write.

At last the mystery man had been found. But there would be another big surprise, four years later.

34

Puzzles

I never did get to meet the third man, Jacques Price. A month after our conversation I sent him a copy of Stanley Handman's 1953 *Weekend* magazine article. I thought it might kindle other memories about Whitehead. But Price never answered the accompanying letter. During the next couple of years I phoned him several times trying to set up a meeting and, although usually polite, he never seemed particularly enthusiastic to cover that ground again.

In 1992 I booked a trip to Halifax. When I called him from Sutton a few days before the planned departure to make sure he'd be there, he said in a charged voice that he was at his wit's end. His wife had pancreatic cancer and she had had two strokes. This was not the time to come.

In 1994 I applied for a Canada Council grant to start writing this book. As an afterthought I asked for transportation costs to Halifax. In July, before hearing from the Council, I received a surprise phone call from Karen. It had been four years since we had last communicated. She had obtained my phone number from cousin Phil. She and her husband Ian were planning to leave in a few days for England. She was eager to look up the relatives in Preston, and thought I might have Anita's or Hilda's address. She disclosed that her father had died the previous summer. Her mother had passed away several months before him. She revealed that she had never known about this Preston branch of the family until I'd phoned her in 1990. It was like finding her own roots, she said, which she never knew existed.

We touched on the Houdini affair. Karen said she tried bringing up the subject on several occasions after learning, from me, that he had been in Houdini's dressing room. Her father was always reticent to talk about it. He would only say he didn't do anything wrong and that he told Whitehead "You've got to stop! You're going to kill the man!" Again she pointed out that her father was very private, but perhaps after meeting the relatives in Preston she'd find out more about his background.

We spoke again after their trip. She was ecstatic. Although Anita had died and she wasn't able to find Langstrath, they spent an entire day with her Aunt Hilda and cousin Malcolm and his family in Blackpool.

"I was glad to find out there was no falling out with Dad or with the family. And it was amazing how much my aunt was like my father. Just in little ways, the way she expressed herself, her bearing."

In Oxford they stumbled on Ruth Brandon's *The Life and Many Deaths of Harry Houdini*. It had just come out. They were surprised to discover that her father is quoted at length in the book.

I'd heard about it. It is a psychological portrait of Houdini. I picked it up in Montreal. Sure enough, it has four long paragraphs that Brandon attributes to Price ("Jack Price told what happened next ... ") describing the dressing room punch. It was more or less the same as Smiley's version, but worded differently. The source given in the reference notes is Conan Doyle's *The Edge of the Unknown*, published in 1930. But Doyle's rambling essay doesn't mention Price by name. In the first chapter where he claims that Houdini had supernatural powers, Conan Doyle attributes the quote to one of the three students in Houdini's backstage dressing room. Since Whitehead and Smiley are mentioned by name in the quote, it seemed that Ruth Brandon put one and one together and assumed that the student Doyle referred to was Price.

Had Conan Doyle met Price? Not likely, if Price didn't return to England after he dropped out of McGill in 1927. Doyle may have had access to the affidavits that Smiley, Whitehead, and Price were said to have drawn up in 1927. Or he may have concocted the quote. It seems to be more in his own style than that of an eighteen-year-old.

Several months passed. On November 10, the Canada Council grant having come through, I flew to Halifax. Even though Price was deceased, and even though he had related all that he said he could remember, there was still enough mystery about him to warrant the trip and meet his daughter.

35

The Picture

∼

"MY FATHER RECOUNTED the Houdini story very much as you told me," Karen Mann said. We were talking through the din of Down East folk music in the Café Rotterdam on Halifax's Barrington Street. It faces Parade Square where the November 11 Armistice Day activities had just ended. If he'd been alive, Price might have attended the ceremony. He was proud of his time as a flight lieutenant in the RCAF and believed that a well-trained armed force was important to a country's security. He had not served overseas; he was posted in Newfoundland during World War II. The base at Torbay was a transit point for Canadian troops being sent to England. Price's engineering skills in roads, runways, and sanitation helped keep the base running.

These were some of the many details related by Karen Virginia Mann, Price's only child. At the time of the meeting she was associate dean of under-graduate medical education and student affairs at Dalhousie University and mother of three grown children. Appreciative of having made contact with the Preston relatives, she was not opposed to providing some of the missing pieces about her father, although, as she said, she probably couldn't add much to what I'd already learned.

There had been many changes to her life since our conversation in 1990: her parents' deaths, and finding the relatives and "as cliché-ish as it sounds, a lost part of myself" in the English Midlands. Also, she had married Ian Moggs, an associate professor in Dalhousie's Faculty of Medicine's anatomy and neurobiology department.

"I don't know why he was reluctant to talk about the incident," she said. "As far as I know he never talked about it to my mother either. And I have the feeling he would never have brought it up if I hadn't questioned

Jacques Price with his daughter Karen, Halifax, Nova Scotia.
Photo courtesy of Karen Virginia Mann

An older Jacques Price.
"It's amazing. Your father is the spitting image of, well, Harry Houdini!"
Photo courtesty of Karen Virginia Mann

him about it after receiving your phone call in 1990. Whether he thought there might be some criminal action that would arise out of it. The first thing he said to me when I asked him about it was, 'I didn't do anything wrong.' Or whether he thought that it would reveal a part of his life that he didn't want people to know about."

Since he had passed away before the Ruth Brandon biography came out, Karen of course couldn't ask him if he'd ever been interviewed by Doyle.

"But I doubt that he ever met him. Although there were some expressions in the quote that sounded like they would have come from my father—the use of the word 'whilst', for instance—most of the passages didn't seem at all like his speech. The book was deceptive because it came out looking like the author knew Price, as if she interviewed him and was using a direct quote, 'Jacques Price said this to me, said that …'

"My father was a brilliant person," Karen continued. "That's not just my view. Interestingly enough, when I met my Aunt Hilda in England, she also commented on it. What she remembered about him was that he had a wonderful gift for numbers. He was the sort of person, if you listed off a bunch of numbers and said, multiply this, take the square root of that, divide, multiply by twenty-nine, he would be able to do the whole problem in his head. He had an amazing mental agility. He could remember virtually anything. Which is why he had such finesse in bridge. He still remembered Latin when I was growing up and spoke French fluently, absolutely fluently, a classical Parisian French which I think he learned as a young person.

"He was quite a serious man, but had a good sense of humour. He was also very affectionate. He loved his grandchildren. But he had quite swinging moods. I regarded him as in conflict, not always a happy sort of man. And from what I know now, that makes sense to me. Having a secret is always very deceptive."

When she found his birth certificate in his effects after he died, it confirmed that he had been born in 1908, on April 30, which would put his age at eighteen when he entered McGill in 1926. It was not a mistake on the McGill card, as I'd previously conjectured.

"People have their reasons for saying they are older or younger than they are."

Her father and mother met when he was studying at the University of Toronto. "My mother was a secretary to the general manager at the head office of Canadian Imperial Bank of Commerce or whatever it was called then. She was from a very puritanical Anglican Ontario family which probably never would have accepted my father if his background had come out.

"My aunt told me that when my dad left for America it was as a volunteer to help an aunt with seven sons who was emigrating. The aunt really wanted one of the girls, Anita or Hilda, to accompany her, but they weren't interested. My father was only too glad to sail with them, to be their chaperon. Hilda said she thought they landed in Boston. But it didn't seem to work out because he didn't stay with the aunt for very long. And apparently he had money problems when he arrived, and had to write to the family asking for help. Then two years later he turned up in Montreal, at McGill. What happened to the aunt and her sons? I don't know.

"At first he planned to study medicine, but, according to Hilda, after dropping out of McGill he decided to take up engineering at the University of Toronto."

Did her father have any friends in whom he might have confided about the Houdini incident?

"I'd bet my bottom dollar that he never had a friend that was close enough to confide in. He had friends, and a lot of people liked him, but as I told you, he was a private man. To the extent that he confided in anyone, it would have been my mother. She knew his middle name was Isadore. So maybe she knew more than I thought."

Karen suggested contacting the former dean of medicine at Dalhousie, Dr. Chester Stewart, who knew her father from bridge and the Rotary Club. They had been in the RCAF together. I called the next morning, but he said Price had never mentioned the Houdini episode to him.

Was her father interested in the psychic or paranormal realm, I asked. Could he have known Whitehead or any of the spiritualists?

"Oh God, no. He was very down to earth, pragmatic, but a thinker as well. He read news magazines every week of his life, and watched the news and current affairs programs religiously. He loved conversation, talking about world affairs. He was very interested in finances, the stock market. Later in life when he started to go deaf it was frustrating for him because he couldn't hold up his end in conversations."

We left the café and drove to the house on Quinpool Road where Price lived from the time of his retirement in 1966 until he died. It is a charming white 100-year-old wood-frame cottage near the North West Arm inlet. It had once been owned by Sir Charles Tupper, Prime Minister of Canada for ten weeks in 1896, former Nova Scotia premier, and one of the Fathers of Confederation. In back was a sprawling sloped lot. "In the early years when they lived there, my mom had a beautiful garden on the grounds in the back," Karen said as she posed to have her photo taken in front of the house.

The muses' special magical coincidence took place after we drove back to Karen's home in the South End; while we were having coffee, Ian brought down a box of family photos and mementos from the attic.

We were looking through them with Karen's daughter Gillian. Here was a photo of Jacques Price, four years old, with Hilda; another of him in his RCAF uniform; another of Price with Karen when she was a little girl …

And then an eight-by-ten framed portrait photo. Price in his early fifties.

"That's not your father!"

Karen and Ian were looking at me because I suddenly had, again, that being hit off-guard *wamblecroft* expression of dismay.

"But … but, I can't believe it! Can't you see it?"

They couldn't, or were too close to Jacques Price to notice.

"It's amazing. Your father is the spitting image of, well, Harry Houdini!"

The man in the photo had the same broad receding forehead and short plastered-down wavy hair with an incursion on the left where the hair splits and the part begins, the same indented frown line over the eyes, the same arching heavy eyebrows thinning as they moved down toward the edges, the same deep-set eyes with the corners squeezed and a trace line directly underneath each, the same aquiline nose with a pleat on each side flaring off from the nostrils toward the mouth, the same straight lips with little pockets at each end, the same rounded jaw, and, eerily, the same look.

36

The Doctor's Wife

HALIFAX HAD ONE MORE amazing "coincidence" in store. When cousin Phil picked me up Sunday morning in front of the Fresh Start Bed & Breakfast, he had just come from a tennis workout. His partner, Lloyd Newman, was in the front of the car. Lloyd was from Detroit originally. When I told him about the Houdini research, he perked up.

"I've always been interested in Houdini because his doctor was our family physician in Detroit and in fact pulled my tonsils out. Dr. Danny Cohn. I remember thinking he used a shoehorn to yank them. My parents always told me proudly that he was Houdini's doctor and been at Houdini's bedside when he died."

I could only find one mention of Dr. Cohn. It was in Milbourne Christopher's biography. Cohn is named as the house physician at the Statler Hotel who examined Houdini when he returned to the hotel after collapsing at the Garrick Theatre. His name also showed up in an extract from Houdini's memorial service on the wall at the Houdini Hall of Fame in Niagara Falls, Ontario (which unfortunately would burn down in 1995). He was named as the young physician on call at the hotel who examined Houdini at three in the morning and then summoned the Detroit surgeon Dr. Charles S. Kennedy.

Now, sixty-eight years later, a couple of thousand miles away, my cousin's tennis partner shows up, a Haligonian who had his tonsils removed by the same doctor who told Houdini he required hospitalization.

With the help of Lloyd's family, Dr. Cohn's widow, now Mrs. Ethel Schatz, was traced to an address in Los Angeles. "She is the only (and closest) living link to Houdini's doctor," Phil wrote, after he had obtained the address from his tennis partner. "She is elderly, obviously, and probably quite lucid."

I wrote to Mrs. Schatz, describing the chance meeting with her late husband's tonsillitis patient in Halifax. After telling her about the work on this book, I asked if she could recall her late husband ever telling her about treating Houdini; especially while Dr. Cohn was at Houdini's bedside, had Houdini, in spite of his pain and suffering, said anything to him "about the blow that had caused his injury, about the student, about how he was hit, or about the spiritualists."

Mrs. Schatz graciously wrote back on April 25, 1995, stating that her late husband "often spoke about his experience with Houdini and I'd be glad to relate whatever he told me." Her letter continues,

> J. Gordon Whitehead, the McGill student who punched the great magician in the stomach several times, did so before Houdini had time to flex his muscles. I doubt that anyone, at that time, considered the possibility that he might have done so deliberately but now that you mention it, it certainly seems like a plausible theory to me. Daniel knew nothing about Whitehead other than that he attended McGill, that he was older than the average student, and that he walked into Houdini's dressing room and asked if it was true that Houdini could withstand abdominal blows without injury. He barely waited for a reply before he struck Houdini numerous times.
>
> I'm sure you know that there was a difference of opinion in the medical profession at the time about whether ruptured appendix could be caused by abdominal punches. Daniel absolutely believed Houdini's death was caused by the blows he had received, and all the doctors on the case concurred so that the New York Life Insurance Company paid Bess Houdini double indemnity.
>
> I wish you luck in your endeavour. ... It gave me great pleasure to know that Lloyd Newman mentioned my Daniel as having been his family's physician.

I had further letters, all flawlessly typed, from Ethel Schatz. Almost eighty, she still did some teaching and counselling and was active and obviously very lucid. "I hasten to respond because I'm so enthusiastic about your theory concerning Houdini's death," she started one of her letters.

She wrote that she had met and married Dr. Danny Cohn in 1937. "I was teaching school in Florida and was introduced by two of my students to their bachelor uncle, a physician in Detroit. Daniel was 35 and I was 21. We had three children and now, nine adult grandchildren, three of whom are named after him. … Daniel died in 1970, the saddest day of my life. I married Theodore Schatz in 1977 and we moved to Los Angeles. He developed Alzheimer's and died in 1990."

In Daniel's papers she found one of his scratchpads "where Danny scribbled short memos about his patients." One notation cryptically stated: "Mr. Harry Houdini—magician and author—Strep. Peritonitis resulting from ruptured appendix. Blow received in Montreal on Oct. 22 was exciting factor." Quite likely her husband had written a full case history, she said, "but it would have been on file at the Grace Hospital, which is no longer in existence."

She also found two letters from Bess Houdini's lawyers, the first asking Dr. Cohn for a certified copy of the death certificate, the second asking if his opinion coincided with that expressed by Dr. Charles Kennedy and the other physicians who treated Houdini—"We naturally want to be sure"—that the blows struck in the dressing room at the Princess Theatre were directly responsible for Houdini's death. Dr. Cohn did concur. The package she sent included a copy of a letter from Hardeen, Houdini's brother, thanking the twenty-five-year-old doctor who had just completed his residency at Grace Hospital "for your untiring efforts in behalf of my brother. I can but faintly express the deep gratitude of the members of his family."

Dr. Cohn never kept a journal or wrote family letters about being at Houdini's deathbed, "but he frequently spoke about his experience with the magician because it had such a profound effect on him," Mrs. Schatz wrote. She herself published an article in the *Oakland Sunday Magazine* Halloween 1987 issue, describing how her husband, "an awestruck young novice became friend and confidant to a dying magician." She told how he was called in to see Houdini because an older colleague, leaving on vacation, had asked Daniel to substitute for him at the Statler. He had

Ethel Schatz and Dr. Danny Cohn.
Cohn was the house physician at Detroit's Statler Hotel who
examined Houdini when he returned to the hotel after collapsing at the
Garrick Theatre.

just started his private practice, "and with few patients of his own yet, complied with enthusiasm."

"After Houdini's operation," she wrote,

> innumerable medical men were called in consultation to treat him. They were all well-established outstanding physicians with many patients of their own. Only one young physician had nothing but time.
>
> Daniel welcomed the opportunity to spend night and day at Houdini's bedside, listening every evening to his halting sentences as he reminisced, mostly about his childhood.

She even described in the article how Houdini, although he had no appetite for food, said to her husband one evening that he had "a yen for Farmer's Chop Suey, a favourite dish in Jewish homes, consisting of raw vegetables combined with sour cream." Daniel walked over to a nearby delicatessen and brought two portions and had a kind of last supper with Houdini in the hospital room.

Once again, I pressed Mrs. Schatz in a letter, asking if she could remember anything Houdini might have told Daniel on his deathbed about Whitehead or the punches that Whitehead delivered or the circumstances of the punches.

She reiterated that Whitehead "had not given Houdini time to flex his muscles but had punched him in the stomach as soon as he asked if he could withstand abdominal blows," and added, most pertinently because it bolsters the wilful assault theory, "I also recall Daniel saying that Whitehead kept punching even after Houdini flinched."

37

The Word

∾

ONE DAY IN THE SUMMER of 1995 I drove up to the Mount Royal Cemetery and asked to look at the Whitehead death certificate. It had been nine years since Edith Knowles had found his card in the cemetery files, the card containing the clues that resulted in his being traced. Perhaps it would have a word about Whitehead's cause of death that she had overlooked.

Edith Knowles had retired, but the cemetery's administration co-ordinator, Jo-Ann Harding, found the forty-one-year-old registration card, number 149620, bleached with age. It offered only the word "Natural" beside the space for "Cause of death," which, back in 1986, is what the Queen Elizabeth Hospital's then director of professional services, Dr. Eric Phelps, had also said. Dr. Phelps had given me the name of the physician listed in the hospital's registry as having treated White-head: Dr. Finley McMartin. But the cemetery's card clearly showed, as Edith Knowles had said at the time, that it was Dr. John McMartin, Finley's brother, who had signed the death certificate.

John McMartin was still working in Montreal as a general practi-tioner. He said over the phone that he had no recollection of Whitehead. Could that be, I asked, because he had never treated him, or because it was too far back for a doctor to recall just one patient among thousands?

"It could be either," Dr. McMartin said. But he thought if he'd known that one of his patients had been involved with someone as famous as Houdini, it was very likely he would remember him.

"But the name doesn't ring a bell. I'm sorry."

I now had a contact in the Queen Elizabeth Hospital and using his name and emphasizing the importance of the research, I pressed again to have access to the hospital's files, pointing out that Whitehead had no near next-of-kin and that although personal information about a medical condition may be deemed private, it was only the cause of death I was interested in, something which is usually given in newspaper obituaries in any case. Since Dr. Phelps had retired, there were others who were now in charge of the files and patient information.

One day I found myself in the basement records department speaking to an obliging archivist who said the hospital would see what it could do. But probably there wasn't much she would be able to find out, she said, because there had been a fire in the hospital in 1956 and all the doctors' and nurses' reports prior to that date had been destroyed.

However, the registry book still existed and, yes, she said after scrutinizing it, a cause of death was given.

"You mean natural?"

"There's another word."

"What is it?"

"I can't tell you."

"Can't you just whisper it?" I bent over, hoping she would murmur the one word in my ear. "I won't tell anyone," I promised, speaking low so no one else in the records room would hear.

"I can't. You'll have to sign a form and then it will have to be cleared with the hospital administration."

I signed the form.

"We'll phone you in a few days."

The following week, the message finally came. On the answering machine was the sweet voice of the hospital archivist saying "just to let you know that we have your information. We are able to give it to you, so if you want to come and pick it up or if you want us to mail it to you just call us back to give us your address, otherwise you can come whenever. Thank you. Bye-bye."

I could have phoned straight back to ask her to pronounce the word on the phone, now that the green light had been given, but that seemed, well, unmomentous, so instead I bounced into the car and burned up the road driving the 100 kilometres into Montreal to learn the secret death word.

The envelope, please—

In response to your inquiry 3 – 5 – 95,
requesting information on the above named, we are pleased
to provide you with the cause of death.
This information was taken from the hospital registry book.

Cause of death: <u>MALNUTRITION</u>

Trust this information will be assistance to you.

Malnutrition.

38

Hunger

∽

I SHOWED THE RODICK PHOTO of Whitehead to Dr. William Barakette, a general practitioner working out of Cowansville in Quebec's Eastern Townships who had seen just about everything in his twenty-five years of family medicine. What would his first impression have been if this tall man had walked into his office?

"When you see somebody like this, very thin with gaunt features, you immediately think heavy smoker, and ulcer problems. The taut features also make me think of lung or stomach disease.

"Any one of these might have caused the eating disorder, the malnutrition, that killed him. He could have had a cancer of some sort, lung or stomach cancer, which wouldn't necessarily have been diagnosed at the time. They would not have known if that was the underlying cause of the disease unless they had done an autopsy. Unless you cut someone open to determine what it is, or if you do all the blood tests, it's hard to tell. The state of inanition, or total wasting, that you see in the end-state cancer is malnutrition, so it's most likely, if it wasn't clear, that they just put down that one word as cause of death.

"But it could well have been some other factor. People whom I've seen die of malnutrition—men of that age—the most common cause is alcoholism. It could be that by the time he arrived at the hospital he developed cardiomyopathy, a disease of the heart muscles from malnutrition that could be linked directly to alcohol. Back then they weren't diagnosing alcoholism as such. They wouldn't flat out write 'Alcoholism' as cause of death, but it could well have been that."

There had never been any indication from anyone I interviewed that Whitehead was an alcoholic or heavy drinker.

"Another possibility is some kind of narcotics addiction. Opium, heroin, cocaine—any of these could have affected his appetite. It's only speculation, but this might also explain the events in Houdini's dressing room. If he had a drug problem, say, which pre-existed, then you can imagine—he was very strong, as you mentioned—he needed money for cocaine, or even alcohol, whatever the addiction was it had to be satisfied. Thus he might have been paid a fee, and of course went on and continued to use throughout his life whatever the substance was that he craved."

I remembered Ivie Miller's story of the packages left at the door of Whitehead's apartment and the mysterious callers. "The question arises," Ivie Miller had said, "did Mr. Whitehead do drugs? He looked like a man who conceivably did take drugs."

"The rash on the face [which Jack Rodick had noticed] is also interesting," continued Dr. Barakett. "There is a disease called lupus erythematosus—which means 'redness'—that produces a butterfly distribution rash over the bridge of the nose which can also induce a state of malnutrition through loss of appetite because all the organ systems have become affected, and the brain can become affected too—you can develop a lupus dementia when the person becomes confused and there's kidney failure, which is generally what kills them."

Other possibilities?

Celiac disease, Crohn's disease, Whipple's disease—all of which affect the digestive system or gastrointestinal tract and can bring on serious nutritional malfunctions.

"But without seeing the medical reports, you couldn't really pinpoint the underlying condition causing the malnutrition that killed him. All we can do is take educated guesses."

Was anorexia nervosa, a willed decision not to eat, a possibility? Had Whitehead arrived at the "joyful insanity hunger was," according to novelist Knut Hamsen, which made him "empty and free of pain?"

"Not likely in a man that age," the physician responded. "Anorexia suggests a broader picture of depression. He could have been depressed, as you say, because he privately carried the Houdini incident with him his entire life, but it's doubtful that that alone would have made him anorexic or that he would have just stopped eating.

"It's unusual for somebody to starve himself to death because he has killed somebody. More likely, you have to ask, and now I come back to my earlier thought, did he take recourse in some kind of drug because killing Houdini left him with this life-long depression? But even then, for perpetrators of that kind of act, ordinarily there's a psychopathic element. They don't have feelings or remorse, especially if they did something to somebody else because of belief, or for a fee."

But to know how the Houdini incident might have affected Whitehead's state of mind, and by extension his health, "you would be better off," Dr. Barakett said, "to speak to a psychiatrist."

I contacted the man he recommended, Dr. Pierre Gagné, a well known forensic psychiatrist attached to the University of Sherbrooke. We made an appointment to meet in a few days.

39

Shrink's-Eye Views

∼

"Looking at the photo," said Dr. Pierre Gagné, a well known forensic psychiatrist connected with McGill and the University of Sherbrooke who works closely with police, parole boards, and courts assessing criminal personalities, "he could be almost anybody—a police officer, a detective, somebody you meet on the street."

We were discussing Whitehead in the psychiatrist's medico-legal clinic in downtown Sherbrooke, Quebec. Long svelte couches dominated the spiffy consultation room. The walls were covered with photographs of whales. I had briefed him about the Whitehead punches and brought out the bookstore photo of the puncher.

"It's difficult to create a character profile of someone without speaking to them for a few minutes, which of course we can't do," he said, examining the picture.

"At first sight, he's obviously interested in intellectual matters. He doesn't look like someone who doesn't take care of himself. He's well-dressed, he's wearing a shirt and tie, his hair is trim.

"It would be interesting to know more about the steel plate in his head," the practitioner continued. "If he'd had a frontal lobe injury and brain damage, it could have affected his judgment. As you say, we don't know whether he had the accident before or after he punched Houdini. It would be more interesting if he had it before. If he'd had brain damage, it wouldn't have been the only incident where violent or irrational behaviour was evident. There might have been recurrences. It's too bad we don't have access to his medical charts to find out if he was ever treated for psychiatric problems."

Could Dr. Gagné guess what Whitehead's state of mind might have been when he was in Houdini's dressing room in 1926?

"Well, we can guess in several directions. If this is a normal person we are talking about who had injured Houdini accidentally by delivering a punch in reply to Houdini making a speech, saying 'I can sort of collect my muscles to the point where I will not feel any pain'—unless you're dealing with a very immature person, he would have said, after realizing that he'd injured the magician, 'Oh my God, what have I done?' and made sure an ambulance or doctor was called. He would have stayed there and looked concerned and have tried to do something to repair the damage. At least he would have apologized. He wouldn't have kept striking Houdini to further test his resistance.

"On the other hand, if he had something personal against Houdini or was a professional hit man, say, working for the mediums or whomever, and did it intentionally, he wouldn't have said anything. He would have just walked away quickly and tried to escape prosecution by disappearing—fast. Especially because there were witnesses. And he would have lived in constant fear that the truth would come out and he'd be charged.

"There is also, as you say, the possibility of drugs, but I doubt very much that he would have been so spaced out, so stoned that he wouldn't have known what he was doing. It wasn't extremely common in those days for people to take substances, like cocaine, say, just to uplift their mood. Opiates weren't so widespread as they are now and weren't taken in the same dosages and didn't have the same psychological effect. Also, from what you tell me, it seems like he knew very well what he was doing.

"What you said about him living like a hermit is interesting. He could have had a mental disorder, he could have been schizophrenic, although it's unwise to jump to the conclusion that somebody who lives like a recluse is necessarily a schizophrenic. Many schizophrenics when they don't get treatment of course do end up in pathetic conditions living as misfits and hermits, but sometimes hermits are simply that, choosing a style of life totally cut off from mankind without necessarily having any of the thought disorders that you find in schizophrenics.

"But if he was insane to a certain degree, the incident with Houdini would have made him more insane, more withdrawn. Considering how he ended up, his apartment full of soot and newspapers as you tell me and being isolated and secretive and starving himself to death and then with that steel plate in his head, we can certainly presume he was suffering from some kind of mental disorder. It's not impossible. And then if that was true, you can elaborate all types of theories—especially if the insanity already existed when he had the episode with Houdini.

"He could have been having hallucinations, or felt he was fulfilling a mission, real or unreal. He may have been hearing voices. Although I've never seen a case anything like this, it's known that sometimes you can be in the presence of a schizophrenic and if they aren't being treated, they may suddenly, out of the blue, attack you and say, 'Well, somebody told me to do it'—an inexplicable aggressive action, totally irrational to us.

"But let's say he was sane and rational and for whatever reason wanted to kill Houdini, that we're dealing with a non-psychiatric type of murder," Dr. Gagné went on. "In my opinion, he wouldn't have done it this way. First of all, it's not something known to kill people, to punch them in the abdomen, even if we do it several times. How could he have known that nine days later Houdini would be dead?

"And even if he had intended only to hurt him, assuming we're dealing with a 'normal' intelligent person—intelligent because he was a university student—why would he have done it in front of other people? Why wouldn't he have waited until he could catch Houdini alone? In those days even a star like Houdini was not accompanied by bodyguards."

"The point being—?"

"The point being—let's suppose he was so-called normal and had malicious intentions. I don't think it's the way he would have struck, which makes me believe that perhaps he was influenced by people, and the crazier he was, the easier it would have been to influence him. If we use the argument that he was involved with some kind of spiritualist cult or sect, by being abnormal, or a little bit paranormal, it would explain why he did it, out of the blue, in front of witnesses."

"Maybe," I suggested, "he didn't realize there would be others in the dressing room—Sam Smiley and Jacques Price—and expected to find Houdini alone."

"Oh, I know. But if he had been a careful criminal, he would have found an excuse, come up with a stupid little story, would have left and waited for another opportunity. But if he was a little unbalanced, he would not have been careful. And the more unbalanced he was, the less careful he would have been. He was terribly careless, which makes me think that there was something wrong with him. He could have had hallucinations or developed delusions, especially about Houdini. He may even have gone after him more than once. He could have been in that gang at the Prince of Wales Hotel, if we could prove that an attack actually took place there. It's possible that somebody really did tell him to go after Houdini.

"I keep coming back to the steel plate embedded in his skull. In those days they used metal routinely and would put it in right after a fracture to protect the skull, to prevent pieces of chipped bone from sinking in; they didn't have the materials and procedures we have now. But if there had been a fracture, there could have been brain damage, which would have influenced his behaviour."

I interrupted the good doctor to say that if Whitehead had such brain damage, it would defeat the argument that he was out to get Houdini, that he battered him on behalf of the fraudulent mediums or even just because he took exception to Houdini exposing the fraudulent mediums. Wasn't he suggesting that it was only because of his mental confusion, his being unbalanced, that he delivered the killer blows?

"No. It doesn't defeat the argument at all. Just the opposite in fact. It would explain why he was vulnerable, perhaps to suggestions. And why he could have been used by somebody who wanted to hurt Houdini. He could have been gullible, easily persuaded. The idea to go after Houdini could have been implanted in his head—like the steel plate. That's why it would be so interesting to find out what section of the brain was affected by the accident. Then we could say, 'Look, he was a candidate for spiritual conversion,' you see."

The perspective of a psychoanalyst is rather different. Dr. Michel Dansereau practises in Montreal. He put forward the hypothesis that for Whitehead, Houdini was a father image, and so, rather than trying to argue with Houdini on an intellectual level when they were in the dressing room, which he couldn't do because Houdini his father was a much stronger thinker than he was, Whitehead presented his thoughts with his hand, so to speak, using his fist instead of his head, the punches having such argumentative power that they even incidentally happened to kill Houdini.

"It was as if he was saying, 'Here is my point of view. Maybe I can't keep up with you intellectually, father, but this argument now is smooth and in my mind logical and you have no defence against it.' "

Dr. Dansereau thought it was interesting that Whitehead's brother said that Gordon had taught him "so much about living"—to be a sophisticate and a gentleman.

"It's like he wanted to be a gentleman and teach others to be, but when he met Houdini instead of acting like a gentleman he conducted himself like a wild beast. It's possible that the image he was trying to project of himself as a polite, mannered, sociable person concealed a 'brutalité profonde' which exploded against father. To know more about the source of this, we'd have to explore his family background. All we can do now is hypothesize."

One scenario suggested by Dr. Dansereau was that a complex Oedipal drama was being acted out.

"The wish to kill your father, as in the Oedipal myth, is present in everyone, but it's a subconscious desire—Oedipus killed Laïus during an encounter on the path from Delphi, being provoked, not knowing of course that it was his father he attacked. In a similar way, Whitehead may have subconsciously felt provoked by the father Houdini when Houdini boasted about his stomach muscles and his ability to absorb pain, and it was his destiny to slay him, in spite of himself, not at the meeting of the three roads like in the Greek myth, but at the Princess Theatre in Montreal. He wanted to be stronger than his father, to subjugate him, hence he would throw these ferocious punches with no restraint or moderation. One of the students would scream out, 'For God's sake, stop!' which is also part of the Oedipal context. For the love of the father, stop killing him! If you love him, stop! And perhaps like Oedipus, Whitehead also subliminally conspired to have his mother eventually to himself.

"The fact that he never married, never became a father himself," Dr. Dansereau continued, "is also revealing because of the battering he gave Houdini. You don't have guilt unless you love somebody—it exists only when there's the ambivalence of love and hate. So if he's experienced profound guilt or shame after he's slain Houdini the father, as part of his self-inflicted punishment—subconscious, of course—he would have had to renounce the possibility of ever being joined to a woman and becoming a father himself, like an invisible voice was telling him, 'That's what you want [children], but that's what you can never have.'

"It seems clear from what you're telling me that Houdini loved his own mother more profoundly than his wife. Whitehead may have inden-tified with Houdini in this Oedipal love story, which is like a 'roman d'amour.' He may have recognized himself in the drama and felt part of it. His interest in Houdini may even, though again subconsciously, have been part of a homosexual background, which too would explain why he never married any of the many women he seemed to be courting.

"But we can also take the Oedipus myth as it concerns Whitehead off in a complementary direction. In murder stories, we always say, 'Cherchez la femme.' It's possible that for Whitehead, Houdini repres-ented not only the father image, but, behind that, or maybe rather than that, a mother image, so much so that when Whitehead thrust his fist into Houdini's stomach, he was also trying attacking the stomach of his mother. What was he trying to do? Did he subconsciously wish to destroy the uterus, the maternal womb, the future newborns? Was he jealous of his younger brothers and sisters who might issue from Houdini his mother's womb? Was he trying to kill his unborn self?"

He wondered if Whitehead might not have had a difficult relation-ship with his own real mother, from breast-feeding onward.

"It may have brought about this plight of self-punishment whereby he eventually starved himself to death, which most certainly had psychosomatic origins. He may have had a desire to destroy not only his mother's womb—thus the Houdini punch to the stomach—but also eventually to annihilate himself through the stomach, it being the path of self-destruction most meaningful to him because of his suppressed guilt. The stronger the negation or denial of guilt, the stronger the possi-bility that the guilt will express itself indirectly in physical symptoms. He killed Houdini through the medium of the stomach, and years later, cause of death: malnutrition, you see. A stomach problem."

40

The Missing Affidavits

~

"MR. BELL, you've hit the jackpot!"

It was Christine McKay, an archivist working part-time with the New York Life Insurance Company.

In July of 1995, the writing of *The Man Who Killed Houdini* nearing completion, or so I thought, I decided to make one more attempt to find those mysterious affidavits. Surely one of the insurance companies which had settled with Bess Houdini would have them in their files, if they had in fact existed.

One of the letters Ethel Schatz had copied for me from Dr. Cohn's files was from the Detroit Branch Office of New York Life. It was dated December 17, 1926, and it was regarding Beatrice Houdini's double indemnity insurance claim. The company asked him to fill out a statement about the contributory causes of death since he had attended Houdini.

When I started this research in 1982 and wrote to New York Life trying to track down the affidavits, the company had replied that it "cannot provide the photocopies you have requested of the affidavits of the three McGill students." The then senior archivist, Pamela Dunn Lehrer, suggested contacting the three other insurance companies that paid off claims—Union Central Life, Fidelity Mutual Life, and Metropolitan Life. None of these companies could locate copies of the affidavits. From the New York Life Insurance Company's words "cannot provide," I had concluded that the company did not have the affidavits. Either they were lost or destroyed, or their files did not go back that far, or there never had been any such documents.

But now I wondered if the company might still have a Detroit office and, if so, whether the Houdini file might still be sitting there.

I discovered the company did have an office in Detroit, but nothing in its files on Houdini. A clerk in the records department said if there was anything at all on him it would be in New York. That route had of course been covered in 1982, but he gave me a phone number so I decided to try again.

Jim Tolve, the company's New York media relations consultant, said that they normally kept celebrity files. Surprisingly, he sounded hopeful that something could be found. He said he'd make some inquiries and phone back. Eventually, I got a call from Christine McKay, who had been hired to put some order into the company's documents for its 150th anniversary. Material that had once been stored away and next to impossible to track down was now accessible. She said she'd see what could be found on Houdini, but cautioned that even if something turned up, the company's lawyers might stand in the way of releasing the documents. She asked for details of the students, the correct spellings of their names. Were they deceased? When did they die? Did they have next-of-kin who were still alive? What were my own credentials? This was Thursday, August 3, 1995. A most congenial lady, intrigued by the project, Chris said she would get back to me as soon as possible, probably that same afternoon.

At three o'clock, the phone rang.

She had traced the company's Houdini file and in it found five affidavits from the three students—two each from Smiley (then Smilovitz) and Price, and one from Whitehead. They were two or three legal-sized pages long, typed and notarized. Price and Smiley, it seemed, felt obliged to write second affidavits to correct statements made by Whitehead in his, to specify the number of punches struck and, most crucially, to emphasize that Houdini hadn't prepared himself to receive the punches. The blows had caught him by surprise. It is possible that Mrs. Houdini's lawyers encouraged Smiley and Price to be more precise on this point, since if it was shown that Houdini has solicited Whitehead's punches to demonstrate how firm his stomach muscles were, it would hardly be deemed an accident or an ambush.

She said the file also contained documents and memorandums

relating to Houdini's insurance policies going back many years, affidavits from four members of Houdini's entourage concerning the state of Houdini's health prior to receiving the blows and the distress he experienced afterwards, and letters by five Detroit doctors, including Dr. Cohn, who treated Houdini and who, it would seem, were in agreement that the blows to the abdomen were what precipitated Houdini's death.

Chris reported most cheerfully that the company's lawyers had given their assent, so she could release photocopies of the affidavits as long as the material carried the insurance company's stamp; she'd try her best to photocopy everything that was relevant and put it in the mail that same day.

After the conversation ended I had a dampening thought: suppose Whitehead persuasively, vehemently denied that he had it in for Houdini or that there was any malicious intent? The spiritualist conspiracy theory, even the deranged puncher theory, would be delivered a death blow.

We would see what treats the postman would bring.

41

Sweet Potatoes

Eight days later, on August 11, a thick brown manila envelope from New York Life Insurance / "The Company You Keep", arrived at the local post office. It was stamped with big black letters "First Class." I tucked it under my arm, sat down on the terrace of the village restaurant, ordered a coffee, and started to pore over documents that apparently nobody other than officers of the insurance company had ever seen.

On top were letters from the five Detroit doctors. In general, they concurred that, though a rarity, it was possible for a hard enough blow to the stomach to rupture an appendix and cause advanced peritonitis. The term commonly used was "traumatic appendicitis".

Dr. Charles Kennedy, the surgeon, stated that "Heretofore I ... had some doubt as to the actual existence of such a thing ... but in this case there can be no doubt. It is the first case of undoubted traumatic appendicitis which I have ever seen and I can say without qualification that I believe the blow was directly responsible for Mr. Houdini's death."

The other letters were in a similar vein. Dr. George LeFevre, a specialist in postoperative technique who was in Montreal attending a conference and rushed back to Detroit to treat Houdini, wrote colourfully of a case he had once had "where a young man was kicked by a horse over the appendix that caused a ruptured appendix and peritonitis." A similar image was used by Dr. John Watkins who stated that Houdini suffered "a very definite traumatism of the appendix which may, if you please, be compared to a horse kick in the abdomen, and a gangrenous appendix followed this contusion. ... It is the first concrete example to come to my attention in my twenty years of medical practice." Dr. Herbert Hewitt said that "while appendicitis is usually considered a disease caused entirely by bacteria, I believe in this particular case the blow … was directly responsible for the attack." And of course, Dr. Danny Cohn, in the only letter that was handwritten, stated he agreed with Dr. Kennedy that "without any doubt … the blow was the exciting factor or cause in the death of Mr. Harry Houdini."

The package included internal memorandums about Houdini's five policies with the company—the first was taken out in 1906—which were worth $80,325 to his heirs, or $105,325 if the double indemnity accident provision on his $25,000 last policy, taken out in 1924, was paid. Other memorandums, written after his death, dealt with Mrs. Houdini's bid, through Ernst, Fox and Cane, to receive benefits under the double indemnity clause. The question of whether Houdini had died accidentally or whether he had engineered his demise by foolhardily inviting White-head's blows was elaborately debated in these memos by the vice-president and various officers of New York Life.

Then came the riveting affidavits themselves. Four affidavits were submitted by members of Houdini's entourage, dealing with the state of his health before and after the punching incident.

The longest and most detailed was from Sophie Rosenblatt. She identified herself as "a trained nurse engaged in a professional capacity" to take care of Mrs. Houdini when she fell ill from ptomaine poisoning a few weeks earlier in Providence. She declared that from the time she was called in she saw Houdini daily "and during all such time he was in good health and excellent physical condition in all respects" except for the ankle injury he sustained in Albany.

The three others were from: Houdini's first assistant James Collins; Julia Sauer, Houdini's private secretary and a member of the company; and Julia Karchere, a relative of Bess Houdini and a member of the theatrical company.

Collins stated that he had been with Houdini for eighteen years "and assisted him in all performances given by him in vaudeville, theatres, and elsewhere" and, using words similar to Sophie Rosenblatt's, declared that Houdini was in excellent form, was recovering from his ankle injury, "and did not seem to miss a performance after the injury was sustained."

Julia Sauer likewise noted that he "seemed to be in robust health, was extremely active in connection with the various enterprises and so far as I know, was not ill or suffering from any indisposition." She refuted a rumour being spread around that Houdini was ill on the train on his way to Montreal after his performances at Schenectady. "It is not true … that he vomited on the train during this trip or had any stomach ailment or indisposition whatsoever. Neither was he sick or confined to bed at any time during the summer of 1926 as far as I know, and I saw him practically every day during such summer."

Julia Karchere echoed the words of the others, saying it would have been entirely impossible for Houdini to prepare his show had he been ill.

But all four described Houdini as being in severe pain after he was pummelled in the dressing room.

Sophie Rosenblatt:
He stated that it was the first time in his life that blows really hurt him and he twinged. He stated that he was lying down when the blows were struck and that he was not prepared for them. We had supper together. He was continually rubbing his stomach.

James Collins:
The following morning Houdini told me that he had been greatly bothered about the blows … and from that time on he was in bad condition and it was with extreme difficulty that he managed to give the remaining performances in Montreal and the first performance at Detroit.

Julia Sauer:
Upon returning [to the theatre after lunch], we found Houdini in pain and he stated to us that he had been violently attacked a number of times by a student of McGill University. … He stated that he was lying down at the time and intended, of course, to stand up and brace himself and prepare for such blows as might have been delivered, but that while he was actually engaged in reading his mail, and before he had an opportunity to anticipate the striking or blows or to prepare for them, one of the students, possibly because of a

misunderstanding of his remarks, had struck him violently a number of times from a standing position.

Julia Karchere:
Such blows were being delivered in the neighbourhood of his abdomen ... before he had an opportunity to prepare for them and without his knowing that they would be struck while he was reclining and reading his mail.

Lawyer Bernard Ernst offered to obtain similar affidavits from four of Houdini's stage assistants who had been with him in Montreal, but they "would merely be corroborative" of the statements already gathered, he wrote in his summing-up letter to New York Life's general counsel, Louis H. Cooke. Trying to show there was no pre-existing medical problem, he pointed out that he himself "knew Houdini for many years [in 1932 he would co-author *Houdini and Conan Doyle: The Story of a Strange Friendship*] and saw him at least two or three times each week for many months prior to his death and can independently testify to his exceedingly good physical condition and state of health during a period of years prior to his death."

But it was the affidavits of Whitehead, Smiley, and Price—the witnesses—that were of most interest to the insurance company. Sam Smiley's frat-mate Harry Cohen was assigned by Ernst, Fox and Cane to get the three students' versions of the punching episode. One can assume that they told their stories to Cohen who made notes and then drafted the affidavits in a typically legalese style which they then read and signed. Smiley's and Price's affidavits, similarly and at times identically worded, were sworn before a Commissioner of the Superior Court for Montreal, but Whitehead's, dated March 16, 1927, had a notary public stamp and a notary's illegible name affixed to the document. Smiley's and Price's first versions were signed on different days in February 1927, and the new corrected ones on different days in April 1927, a month after Whitehead's had been drawn up and no doubt scrutinized by Mrs. Houdini's lawyers. It appears that a second affidavit clarifying certain of the points was requested also of Whitehead, who didn't comply. In his letter to the insurance company, Berhard Ernst said it was apparent that Whitehead's first statement "is incorrect in many particulars," but he "declined to make [a further statement] for us stating that he had been advised by his attorney not to do so and fearing that there might be some personal liability on his part for having occasioned Houdini's death."

There are many discrepancies and lies in Whitehead's affidavit. My comments are interjected.

I, J. Gordon Whitehead, of the City of Montreal, being duly sworn to depose and say:

1. *I reside at No. 75 Union Avenue [this is crossed out and there is a marginal note, initialled by him, giving a number, which is illegible, on Drummond Street], in the City of Montreal, and am at present employed in the library of McGill University in Montreal;*

[McGill has no record of Whitehead being employed in any of its libraries, but if he had been hired as a casual he wouldn't be found in the personnel files.

In 1926 he was living not on Drummond in downtown Montreal, but, according to the McGill calendar, at 794 Shuter, now called Aylmer and renumbered. Curiously, during the same period Sam Smiley was living at the Sigma Alpha Mu fraternity at 745 Shuter, which means that he and Whitehead were neighbours for at least a year or more. They are listed at the same addresses in the 1925 McGill calendar. Whitehead's rooms would have been across the street and a few buildings away from Smiley's.]

2. *I attended the lecture given by the late Harry Houdini at 5 p.m. on Tuesday the 19th October 1926 in the McGill Union;*

3. *On Wednesday afternoon the 20th October 1926, I called at the Mount Royal Hotel for the purpose of obtaining an interview with Houdini. The answer I received was that I should call again the next day before 10 a.m.;*

[There is serious doubt that Houdini was staying at the Mount Royal Hotel. There was the incident at the Prince of Wales Hotel on McGill College Avenue where most touring vaudeville entertainers stayed. Unfortunately, neither hotel now exists, guests lists couldn't be found, and Houdini's quarters in Montreal are not mentioned in other affidavits, so Whitehead's statement cannot be challenged.]

4. *On Thursday morning the 21st October 1926, I arrived at the Mount Royal Hotel shortly before 10 a.m. and sent my card up to Houdini. The message came back that Houdini had left for the Princess Theatre and would be glad to receive me there;*

5. *I reached the Princess Theatre at 10:45 a.m. and was admitted to Houdini's room. I was there introduced to Samuel J. Smilovitz, who is a student at McGill University, and who was then sketching Houdini. I was also introduced to Jacques Price, who was also present. Mr. Price is also a student at McGill University;*

[Whitehead has the day wrong: it was Friday morning, October 22. All the other affidavits give Friday as the day of the blows.]

6. *Houdini was reclining on a couch and Smilovitz was seated near the foot of the couch about two feet away from Houdini's right foot;*

7. *I sat myself on Houdini's right and about opposite his chest. Price sat immediately on my right;*

8. *After some conversation with Houdini, Smilovitz, Price and I left the room and about ten or fifteen minutes afterwards Smilovitz, Price and I returned to Houdini's room and resumed our former seats;*

[Neither Smiley nor Price mention in their affidavits that they had left the room with Whitehead. Smiley felt Whitehead's presence was an intrusion.]

9. *Houdini got up from the couch and moved about the room, apparently in some pain, and with some inconvenience because of some injury which he said he had sustained shortly before coming to Montreal. He did not go into any details as to the nature of the injury;*

[Smiley and Price say that Houdini was hobbling around and had been attended to by a nurse "in connection with trouble which he had with his foot." Whitehead must have known if he'd been reading the newspapers that Houdini had injured his ankle.]

10. *The conversation was then continued and turned to the question of keeping fit. Houdini remarked that he could duplicate a famous strongman's feat of supporting the pivot of a bridge over which was driven an automobile containing at least five people.*

[According to Smiley and Price, Whitehead was the first to raise the question of Houdini's strength. "My friend and I were not so much interested in his strength as we were in his mental acuteness, his skill, his beliefs and his personal experiences," say both their affidavits. In the 1980s Smiley would use similar words, recalling Whitehead's "impertinent questions", and saying, "I admired not just [Houdini's] physical prowess, but I admired his mind. He had a superior intelligence, no question about it." Neither Smiley nor Price mention an anecdote about supporting an automobile driven over his body.]

11. *I had previously mentioned a book I had read which set forth the requirements of good health, such as the care of the skin, the maintenance of an abdominal muscular corset, and a good digestion;*

12. *Houdini suggested that I feel his abdomen,—his muscles were like a washboard and his abdomen as unyielding as a sandbag. Houdini invited me to hit him;*

[Neither Price nor Smiley say that Houdini had invited any of them to feel his abdomen. Their version: "Houdini stated that he had extraordinary muscles in his forearms, in his shoulders and in his back, and he asked all of us present to feel them, which we did." In the 1980s Smiley would hold to this story: "Houdini wasn't so proud of his abdominal muscles. He told us, 'My back and forearm muscles are like steel.' And we did feel his arms and they were like steel."

Price and Smiley, in identically worded sections of their affidavits, say that it wasn't Houdini but Whitehead who instigated the blows. According to them, he asked Houdini "Whether it was true that punches in the stomach did not hurt him. Houdini answered rather unenthusiastically that his stomach could resist much, although he did not speak of it in superlative terms." Similarly, James Collins states that Houdini told him Whitehead initiated the blows, saying to Houdini, " 'I suppose that you can stand a strong blow in the stomach,' and he replied that he could. ... Before he had an opportunity to make his muscles rigid and properly prepare," Collins states, "the blows had been struck."]

13. At the time, he was reclining in a half sitting position on the couch,— he had taken up this position for the purpose of the sketch which was being done by Smilovitz, and Smilovitz was still sketching him at the time;

14. I stood on the right side of the couch and facing Houdini's head. My right knee was against the edge of the couch and half way between his knee and his waist;

15. Price was seated directly behind me and Smilovitz was seated diagonally behind me and to my right;

[Smiley and Price both place Whitehead on the left rather than right side of the couch facing Houdini's head.]

16. I struck Houdini quite moderately and he smiled and laughingly said, "Why/, hit me." I hesitated and he repeated, "Hit me.";

[Smiley and Price describe them as "very heavy hammer-like blows below the belt." Neither mention Houdini laughingly inviting Whitehead after the first blow. "Why/, hit me" is written thus. If one removes the slash and comma, one can assign a different meaning to the phrase: "Why hit me?"

In his letter to the insurance company, Bernard Ernst points out, "We cannot attribute very great weight to the statements contained in Mr. Whitehead's affidavit as human nature is such that he will naturally and understandingly minimize what he did because of the grievous consequences of his act. … No one wants to think or believe that he was the cause of another man's death and particularly of one of the prominence of Houdini."

Even the insurance company's legal counsel Louis H. Cooke agreed that Whitehead was in a most embarrassing position. In Cooke's memorandum advising the company to admit liability for the accident indemnity of $25,000 he states, "It might be argued with much force that Whitehead's testimony would naturally be such as to place him in the most favorable light in view of the unfortunate outcome of his action."]

17. I struck him a second blow slightly harder than the first,—he gave not the slightest indication of any discomfort at either of the blows. Both blows were struck to the left side of his body and above the navel;

[The appendix is normally on the right. Smile and Price say the blows "fell on that part of Houdini's stomach to the right of the navel and were struck on the side nearest us which was Houdini's nearest side."

However, unlike most persons, in fact Houdini's appendix did lie on the left side. In her affidavit Sophie Rosenblatt, who was in the operating theatre at Grace Hospital when the appendectomy was performed, declares "Houdini's appendix was located as I saw myself on the left side of the abdominal cavity and precisely in the exact spot that he had repeatedly pointed to as the spot at which the blows had been struck at Montreal."

Perhaps Price and Smiley were influenced by Mrs. Houdini's lawyers to say he was hit on the right side. There were, in any case, several blows and they may have landed at several abdominal sites.]

18. I was then standing above Houdini and he was facing me and I struck him with my right hand. This occurred about 12 p.m.;

[Price, giving more details on this point than Smiley, said Houdini stated after he was struck that "he had had no opportunity to prepare himself against the blows, as he did not think that Whitehead would strike him as suddenly as he did and with such force, and that he would have been in a better position to prepare himself for the blows if he had arisen from his couch for this purpose, but the injury from his foot prevented him from getting about rapidly."]

19. Neither Smilovitz nor Price made any comment whatsoever, and in the position they were in at the time they could not see the part of Houdini's body on which either of my blows landed;

[Here is where Whitehead's story is most out of line, on three points, with the versions given by Smiley and Price.

"They could not see": Smiley states, "I was in a position to see what actually took place in this dressing room and saw the blows delivered by Whitehead as well as that part of Houdini's anatomy struck, inasmuch as I was sketching him at the time, and his whole face and body were plainly visible to myself." Price uses similar wording. The dressing room was described as approximately eight feet by ten feet. "We were not more than two or three feet from Houdini's couch," Smiley states.

"Neither ... made any comment": Smiley states, "At the end of the second blow my friend Mr. Price verbally protested against this sudden onslaught on the part of Mr. Whitehead, using the words: 'Hey there, you must be crazy. What are you doing?' or words to that effect, but Whitehead continued striking even after the protests of my friend." Price acknowledges using the same words, adding, "but Whitehead continued striking Houdini with all his strength."

"Either of my blows": Price, in both his affidavits, states "I am certain ...

of at least four very hard and severe body blows, because at the end of the second or third blow I verbally protested against this sudden on-slaught." In 1990 Price recalled that there were "several" blows. In his first affidavit, Smiley states: "I do not remember exactly how many blows were struck. I am sure, however, that at least two hard and deliberate blows were delivered while my friend believes that the student hit the reclining magician at least four times." In his revised deposition, Smiley changes it to "several very hard and severe body blows" and recalls that "Whitehead continued striking Houdini even after the protests of my friend." When he was interviewed in the 1980s, Smiley spoke of "four or five … blows … in rapid succession." Smiley and Price say in their affidavits that "Houdini stopped Whitehead in the midst of a punch with a gesture that he had had enough. At the time he was striking Houdini, the latter looked as though he were in pain and winced as each blow was struck."]

20. The conversation then went on in a general way for about an hour when Mrs. Houdini and one or two attendants came into the dressing room with Houdini's luncheon;

[Both Sophie Rosenblatt and James Collins recall Houdini rubbing his stomach.]

21. At the time Smilovitz had completed his sketch, signed it and gave it to Houdini and the latter thanked him for it;

22. I then left the dressing room and Houdini made some remark to the effect that he had enjoyed our conversation and asked me to call again whenever I liked;

23. Houdini gave me the impression of being a very sick man but his determination to keep going was equally apparent. He insisted on personally dealing with his correspondence in spite of remonstrances from one of his staff, this remonstrance was made in my presence and I accepted it as a hint that I should not continue my conversation;

24. I suggested this to Houdini, but he insisted that I should continue;

25. I called again on Houdini at the theatre on Friday morning the 22nd October 1926 at 10 a.m. During our conversation we spoke of longevity and he gave me a copy of the "Scientific American" for November;

[We have established that the punching took place on the Friday morning. Neither Sophie Rosenblatt nor Houdini's assistants mention a second visit by Whitehead in their affidavits.

I found the November 1926 *Scientific American* at the Atwater Library. The short article on longevity that he mentions is by Albert A. Hopkins and is entitled "How Death Deals Its Cards: Death in a Thousand Shapes is Knocking Eternally at Everyman's Door". It presents U.S. mortality statistics for 1923 by cause of death. It may have interested Whitehead to know that 8.12 percent of total deaths that year, or 98,030, were caused by diseases of the digestive system, and there were 7,878 homicides.]

26. Our conversation was general and there was no particular incident to be noted;

27. I visited Houdini on a third occasion, either later on the day of Friday the 22nd, or on the following day;

28. Our conversation was again of a general character and there is no incident worthy of note. Houdini did not on any of these three occasions refer to the incident of my blows as having incommoded him in any respect, or caused him any harm.

And I have signed
J. Gordon Whitehead

42

Whitehead's Signature

~

I SHOWED WHITEHEAD'S signature to two graphologists in Montreal, without saying who he was.

Both Doris Gauthier (male gender; Doris can be a man's name in French), director of the Institut canadien de caractérologie, and Marie Vanasse, director of the Bureau d'études graphologiques, emphasized that any reading would have to be provisory since a signature alone usually is not enough to work on; it's just one element in a handwriting portfolio.

Gauthier worked out of a heavily oak-panelled instrument-filled office in his residence on St. Denis Street in Montreal's north end. A lecturer and member of various international graphology organizations, he's often called in by the police or courts for his opinion in cases involving possible forged handwriting, and by personnel departments of companies to analyze handwriting specimens of job applicants for clues to their personalities.

"Very legible and straightforward," he began, studying an enlarged photocopied specimen under a magnifying glass, "which suggests that what you see is what you get. There's no lack of self-confidence.

"You can see it's an angular signature, and firm, which means that he is a man of conviction. If he believes strongly enough in something, he wouldn't let anything, not anything, stand in his way. This angular style has a kind of aggressive flourish. All the letters are connected, which suggests a logical mind, or at least someone with a great deal of perseverance.

"More of a doer than a thinker. It's the signature of someone who will take ideas from other people and put them in action. It's essential that he has feedback from others.

"The dot at the end of the signature is most interesting. It's rare to find a dot closing off a name. Usually it's a sign of … what's the word in English? … méprise … yes, scorn."

The same word my wife had used when she first saw the photograph of Whitehead.

He brought the specimen to another table where there was a microscope and slid it under the glass for even closer examination of the lines and flourishes.

"I'm fascinated by the 'J' and the 'G' at the beginning—the way the 'J' starts off clockwise, then abruptly turns counter-clockwise, then the 'G' moves clockwise again. There's this frenzied twirling and dipping back and forth, these curlicues, which suggest—I hope he's not a relative of yours—that he's the kind of person who would do something behind the back of someone else, in an underhand way. You see, there's an underhand movement. It's like he's closing his hand before he starts.

"There's something also about his past that he doesn't like, is ashamed of. Like he has a skeleton in the closet, some dark secret, perhaps from his childhood, but something very important that he's hiding, or hiding from."

"Could it have been his recent past?" I asked.

"You would have to trace back and compare it with earlier signatures to see how it evolves. Factors which change a person's life may also change how he presents himself through his signature." Gauthier cited Napoleon's signature as a famous example; it became confused as he lost power and eventually dwindled to a shrivelled few scratches when he was exiled.

"The first impression you get," Gauthier said, "and which he projects to others, is that he's a man of principle. But the more you look at it, the more you realize that there is something else on his mind behind the outwardly friendly posture, which is the mask that he shows to the world.

"The thing that still fascinates me the most is the way the 'J' and the 'G' twirl and spin around back and forth. I keep looking at them. Most curious, like this." He moved his hands in a kind of stealthy whirlwind gesture. "Going forward, around, and coming back, like he will do something the other party doesn't expect, behind the back. It's like he starts off by giving his hand as somebody trustworthy and honest—anyway on the surface that's how it looks—then suddenly he swings around with this great flourishing double loop, and does something unpredictable, covert, maybe sinister, like he has a hidden agenda. I think this man was very secretive."

Gauthier switched off the microscope light and pulled Whitehead out.

"Who is he?"

I told him. I also showed him Rodick's photo.

"Yes, angular features. And the eyebrows, of course, very thick. Yes, just as I thought. A man who will go to great lengths, any lengths, to fight for his ideas and he will crush anyone who stands in his way."

A few days later I dropped in on Marie Vanasse, a former lawyer conducting her graphology business out of a basement office in suburban Brossard on Montreal's South Shore. I mentioned nothing about who Whitehead was or about her colleague's good work.

Many of her conclusions were the same as Gauthier's; she too cautioned that one signature was not nearly enough to make a complete handwriting evaluation. What were the conditions on the day that he signed his name? Was he wearing glasses? Did the pen write smoothly? Was there a pad underneath or a hard surface? Did the notary tell him to put the dot at the end of his signature?

"So let's assume this is the way he wanted to present himself to the world and his writing was not disturbed by any abnormal factors." She studied it under a magnifying glass and then a microscope. Her language describing the angles, slants, and loops was more technical than Gauthier's.

"Aggressive. That's what the blunted 't' means, the short stroke suddenly coming off from the stem. We also see this in the lower zone, the way he forms his loops. Look at the pressure on the paper. It's like he's slamming his fists on the table and saying 'That's enough!'"

"He had a lot of vitality. The letters are all linked except between the names, which suggests he was a very logical person. He would follow up on his plans. If he had a strong idea and believed in it, he couldn't be easily sidetracked. You can see that on the buckles, the small loops on top of the 'J', the 'G', the 'o', the 'W', the 'h'. He also had a lot of imagination.

"The letters in the middle zone, you'll notice, have different heights—the measurements change drastically—which means that one moment he was very self-assured, but two minutes later had no self-assurance at all. He wasn't a stable person. He would question and evaluate himself all the time. But he had the faculty of linking ideas very logically. You see this in the hyper-link, how he goes to the end of each name without ever lifting the pen. But look at that large 'J' connected to the 'G'. He could follow through on an idea, or a plan, right to the end, systematically, with perfect logic, and be absolutely convincing, but the premise of his idea could very well be faulty. In other words, you couldn't attack his reasoning once it was launched, but the launching pad might have been defective so his logic, however perfect, might be flying off in a bizarre direction."

Marie Vanasse's explanation of the dot at the end of the signature was slightly different from Doris Gauthier's. "It's like Whitehead is saying, 'I've been generous enough. I've already given you everything I have. That's it. It's over now. Period.'" And he did turn down Bernard Ernst's request to be interviewed further about the Houdini affair.

Vanasse saw him as a man who would act on his compulsions. But the slowness in the handwriting style, although as she pointed out Whitehead might have been writing measuredly because it was an official important paper he was signing, suggested he was a person who would make cautious preparations before carrying out his plans. "If he was going to a meeting, for instance, he'd first want to know who would be there, what kind of setting it was—he'd have a strategy. I can see this also in the slant.

"Similarly, if he was going to act out his aggressions, he would plan most meticulously; he wouldn't just spontaneously get into a fight, for instance; he'd have a scheme. It's this blunted 't' which interests me the most. I keep coming back to it, it's really fascinating; it reminds me of the Marquis de Sade's signature; you can see the pressure, the way he rapidly pushed down his pen with the stroke, stabbing just on one side of the 't'—yes, he certainly was a brutal man in a way."

I told her who he was.

"Ah, yes. I'm not surprised. You can see it in the terminals and the club-like strokes, sure signs of extreme ruthlessness, somebody inclined to sudden outbursts which may lead to trouble with the law. Such disturbed pressure is frequently found in the writing of criminals."

43

Bert's Odd Story

~

LATER IN 1995, there was another breakthrough, in the sense that someone else came forward who knew Whitehead fairly well during the last two years of his life. His name was Thomas Albert McConnell, known as Bert to family and friends. He was a seventy-five-year-old Belfast-born retired textile company accountant from the Montreal suburb of Lachine. McConnell replied to a Montreal *Gazette* Halloween column by Peggy Curran about the Houdini project. Peggy had added a footnote saying that I'd be interested in hearing from anyone who knew Whitehead or had information about his death.

McConnell wrote October 6, 1995:

Re J. Gordon Whitehead

Dear Sir,

Having read your article in a recent *Gazette* regarding the above named I am wondering whether it would be wise to "resurrect the dead."

As you probably know by now, Gordon died in the Queen Elizabeth Hospital many years ago and was buried from the Collins Funeral Parlour on Sherbrooke Street West (a Quaker ceremony with very few mourners in attendance). Gordon had lived as a recluse for many years on Sherbrooke Street in Westmount.

If you wish to contact me at the above address or telephone number, please do.

Thomas McConnell

My first thought was—crank. A petulant spiritualist with a dire warning not to "resurrect the dead." But he must have known Whitehead since it hadn't been revealed in any of the interviews about him—there had been several in recent weeks on radio and in the press—that he died in the Queen Elizabeth Hospital or that the funeral service had been at the Collins parlour.

I talked to McConnell briefly on the phone and then we met in his Lachine bungalow. He spoke with a rich Irish brogue. He had immigrated to Montreal around 1950. He wasn't at all a peeved spiritualist. The Lachine man was a level-headed cheery fellow whose main frustration was that his golf outings had been recently curtailed due to worsening arthritis.

There was no mistaking the house. The old model Chevrolet Caprice parked on the street in front had a screaming "God Made the Irish No.1!" plate. A scintillating green shamrock was painted on the paved driveway and a glass shamrock hung on the front door. Even though St. Patrick's Day was long past, McConnell was wearing a green tie.

We went downstairs into the finished room in the basement. The article in the *Gazette*, he said, was the first that he had heard about this Houdini project, otherwise he probably would have stepped forward much sooner. He'd often considered writing something about Whitehead himself, although during the time he knew him, from 1953 until his death in July of 1954, he wasn't aware that he was the person who cuffed Houdini. It was only after reading an article, "The Death of a Magician" by Raymund Fitzsimons in the October 1981 *Reader's Digest* that he made the link between this mysterious eccentric person who hired him to do odd jobs, and Harry Houdini. As for his question about "whether it would be wise to resurrect the dead," he said it was out of concern for Whitehead's family, if he had any, which might have preferred not to have the Houdini punch story made public. McConnell didn't need much coaxing to tell his story.

McConnell had come to Montreal in 1952, and was trying to save up money to bring his family over. Since he had been involved with the Boy Scouts in Ireland, he joined a Rover troop in Montreal. One day when he was looking for work he called Scout headquarters to see if there were any odd jobs available. He got a call back from someone "very high up" in the Sun Life Insurance Company, "perhaps the president", who was involved with the Scouts. Would McConnell be interested in a part-time job, he asked, as he'd received a call from an old McGill friend, name of Gordon Whitehead, who was looking for someone trustworthy to do some odd jobs for him.

Whitehead—this came as a surprise—was living on Sherbrooke Street in the Pickwick Arms, at Marjorie Goldstein's, not on Lincoln. Bert phoned the number that the Sun Life higher-up gave him; he needed the extra money and was prepared to do any work.

Whitehead, speaking slowly and very precisely on the phone, gave him most curious instructions. He told Bert to take the elevator up the fourth floor, where the apartment was located, but to make sure that no one boarded the elevator with him. When he got off, he was to ring the bell—"something in code, like two short rings and two long"—and then wait until Whitehead came to the door.

He did as he was told. He rang using the code and after a while heard creaking footsteps, then the door opened a crack, just enough for White-head's bewhiskered chin to stick through. He lifted the chain latch and opened the door. He was a tall, emaciated-looking man with a gaunt angular face, altogether unkempt with thinning straggly hair and a rough scruffy beard, and wearing tattered and torn trousers.

"He said, 'Mr. McConnell, I don't want you to be shocked. My appearance may not be what you expect. That's why I'm letting you see me before I let you in. You can change your mind of course and not do the job.'"

The apartment was pitch dark. He had a flashlight and shone it ahead of them. Bert's first thought was that it was a practical joke, that the Scout troop was involved, that there was some strange rite in Canada and he was going to be initiated into one of the chapters. He thought the lights would go on any second and half a dozen guys would suddenly step out of cupboards and should "Hurrah!" and pour something fizzy over him.

When they went into the living room, Whitehead turned on a dim lamp. It was a sizable room cluttered with newspapers and magazines

Bert McConnell, 1995.
As a young man, Bert McConnell did odd jobs for Gordon Whitehead
in the last year or two before Whitehead died.
Photo by Don Bell

stacked at least six feet high against three of the walls and dusty books plopped on the few pieces of old furniture and scattered on the floor.

Speaking in the same slow, modulated voice he used on the phone, taking a long time just to say a few words, Whitehead told him that his job would consist mainly of moving the newspapers, magazines, and books around from various piles into other piles or against the fourth wall. He was to refrain from reading anything but should follow his instructions to a "T", lifting and moving things around only as he was told.

"That basically is the job that I will require of you."

"He didn't seem drunk or drugged," Bert said, "but weird, very eccentric."

Whitehead told him he could start next week and he'd be paid two dollars each time he came.

Two bucks of course went further in those days. Bert was working then at Simpson's department store wrapping parcels, earning forty-two dollars a week and sending most of it to his wife and youngsters in Belfast; the only indulgence he allowed himself was to spend twenty-five cents a week on two draft beers (ten cents each and a nickel tip) at the Forum Tavern. Whitehead's two dollars from time to time was like extra pudding topping his restricted financial diet.

From January to June 1953, he made six or seven visits, he recalled, shuffling newspapers around exactly as he was told to do. He was astounded when Whitehead said he hadn't left the apartment in ten or twelve years.

Another bold lie or fantasy—witness the photo in Rodick's book-store late 1940s or early 1950s, and his nightly sorties from the Lincoln Street apartment.

Though it was a well-kept Westmount building, in Whitehead's apartment there was thick dust on all the newspapers and books, on the mutilated old upholstered settee and chairs, on blinds and fixtures. It was always dark. The windows were never opened. There were no pictures to brighten it up. It was humid and stuffy. Bert never saw the bedroom or the bathroom but could imagine they were in the same musty state as the rest of the apartment.

After a while, Whitehead's physical problems became worse—he wasn't eating, was losing weight, couldn't get up to answer the door. When Bert rang using the special code, the door would open a crack, the chain would be lifted off, then he'd hear light scurrying, probably Mabel Jackson, Bert now assumed, hiding in the kitchen. Definitely not overweight Marjorie Goldstein, whom Bert in fact never met until Whitehead's funeral. Whitehead talked to him about Marjorie, saying he was treating her for obesity but she was constantly thinking about food, and would gluttonously gulp down a box of chocolates whenever his back was turned.

When Bert arrived in the sombre, spooky apartment, it was usually straight down to business. He was given instructions: move that newspaper from over there and this one here, on that pile, don't look at them, don't read anything. Whitehead never explained to him why he wanted them shifted around; they didn't seem to be classified by newspapers names, or by date. By subject? Maybe.

Bert also picked up Whitehead's mail in his box at the downtown post at Ste. Catherine and Bishop. Because he thought the mail contained some cheques, Bert had the impression that Whitehead had been a rewrite man or editor, possibly freelancing for the *New York Times*. Many of the newspapers in the apartment were from New York. He had to be getting money from somewhere.

Whether he worked for half an hour or for four hours, Bert would be handed two dollars when the job was completed, and a bottle of Molson Export beer and a cheese sandwich on brown bread with lettuce, "which Miss Jackson must have made because he certainly couldn't move around very much."

Bert's wife and children arrived from Belfast in June 1953. There were only two or three more work sessions in Whitehead's apartment. "I had more or less disassociated myself, and Gordon I think realized I didn't have the time to be at his beck and call." Whitehead helped his wife get a job as a typist at Sun Life, using the same "very high up" contact as before.

He continued to have contact with Whitehead, however. As Whitehead's health deteriorated, Bert would get panicky calls, sometimes in the middle of the night, Whitehead telling him to rush over—"Take a taxi, come over at once." Once he had to leave a party; when he arrived, somebody opened the door ("probably Miss Jackson") and then pitter-pattered into the kitchen; everything in darkness, as usual. He had to feel his way around. He found Whitehead lying flat on his back on the hospital trundle bed he slept on, up against the wall in the living room. He was in pain because of his back and needed help just to be raised. He was obviously too heavy for Miss Jackson, if that's who was in the apartment.

"That's all right, that's fine, now you can go," he groaned after Bert helped him up into a half-sitting position.

Another time he sent Bert in a taxi to Dorval Airport to mail a letter which he insisted leave on the first flight to Britain. It was bizarrely addressed to "The Maker of Stoves", in Esher or East Surrey or "someplace like that". A couple of weeks later there was a reply from the mysterious "Maker of Stoves" and when Whitehead nervously opened the envelope and read the letter, "he seemed very upset—'Oh, God!'—as though he'd just been delivered an awful blow."

Whitehead often sent his odd-job helper to Young's Chinese grocery on Sherbrooke for a size ten or twelve grapefruit, "always blood red. He ate grapefruits, raw vegetables, and very little else." Twice when Mabel apparently was away, Bert brought over the sister of one of his friends who had to chop the cabbage and lettuce up to Whitehead's specifications, so minutely that she told him jokingly if they were chopped any finer he'd find her fingernails in the rapé. He required all of his vegetables to be thinly sliced, possibly because of the condition, whatever it was, that was at the root of his eating disorder.

He never mentioned Houdini. "But he was always very secretive. I always had the feeling that he was hiding from something." At the time, Bert thought it might have been because he had discharged himself from the Montreal General Hospital without paying the bill. But with hindsight, he considered it more likely that he had a dread of history catching up with him because of the Houdini affair.

"He acted all the time as if somebody was after him. I'm sure somebody must have been. I reckoned this must have been the reason he was in seclusion. If I'd known at that time about the Houdini business, I would have been taking notes and paying much more attention to everything.

"If he did what he was supposed to have done, and I presume he did, he may have had remorse, or he may have been just plain scared."

Whitehead talked about himself only in patches. Bert remembers him telling him that he had studied medicine at McGill, also that he had worked as spieler on Montreal tourist buses. And that he hurt his back working on a construction site up north. As a prank one of his co-workers left him hanging on a crane until he couldn't hang on any longer and "he fell quite a distance to the ground."

Was Gordon imitating Houdini? In one of his stunts Houdini had himself bound up and locked into a packing case which was lifted by a crane and dropped into the waters off New York's Battery, and he often used cranes as props.

"He seemed to be well educated, in his own way, not necessarily scholastic. He seemed to know a lot."

One time, Bert remembered, Whitehead expounded on the importance of posture; for good overall health, to avoid backaches, one should always sit upright, on a straight-backed chair. A lot of trouble people have, Whitehead told him, was because they sat in soft chairs and "slooped."

He never met anyone else in the apartment, neither Marjorie nor Mabel. Bert didn't know if he had any friends. But he recalled as Whitehead got ready to be admitted to the Queen Elizabeth Hospital, he instructed him to find a pay phone downstairs and call Lady Marler, "who was living in the Eastern Townships," to let her know that he was being hospitalized. Lady Marler, I would later find out, was the wife of Sir Herbert Marler, a minister in Prime Minister Mackenzie King's government in the 1920s, the first-ever Canadian ambassador to Japan, and later ambassador to the United States. In the family history *Marler: Four Generations of a Quebec* family, I learned that King had been fond of Lady Marler and correspondended with her. Also, she had been friendly with the Jaquays in Sutton, with whom Mabel Jackson would live for two years following Whitehead's death.

He asked Bert to phone Mabel Jackson as well. Whitehead said that he was suffering from oedema (swelling). Bert remembered visiting him in the hospital. "He was a skeleton, all skin and bones. He was conscious but just staring up at the ceiling and not saying anything."

It was a small funeral service at the Collins parlour, with only seven or eight mourners present, including Marjorie and Mabel and the Chinese grocer. It was a Quaker service, "where nobody says anything until the spirit moves you, then you can say your piece." Marjorie and Mabel and the grocer made speeches. Bert didn't, realizing he would just be repeating what the others had already said, that he had found Whitehead to be a gentleman, though very serious and most odd.

There were all of Whitehead's effects to dispose of. Mabel asked him if he knew of anyone with a truck. Mabel, or Marjorie, or both, had bundled up all the old newspapers and junk but it was too much to leave in back of the Pickwick Arms, so Bert borrowed a pickup truck from a friend and, as Mabel instructed, distributed Whitehead's "remains" here, there, and everywhere, all over the back lanes of Westmount.

Gordon had left Bert a number of books, or so he was told by Mabel, who passed them on to him. One was H. van de Velde's classic sex manual *Ideal Marriage*. He also inherited *Neurosis and Human Growth: The Struggle Toward Self-Realization* by Karen Horney, one or two volumes by or about Freud, and a book on obesity. In each he found a crisp American one-dollar bill, placed between the covers like bookmarks. He was also given an old tuxedo, much too large for him, that Mabel told him Gordon wanted him to have. When Bert took it home his wife pointed out, "You know, dear, it's full of moth holes." In the pockets he found an American twenty-dollar bill. He kept the money, threw out the tuxedo, and sold the books to a second-hand bookstore.

44

The Hand and the Mind

THE GRAPHOLOGIST Marie Vanasse saw in Whitehead's signature the club-like strokes of "somebody inclined to sudden outbursts which may lead to trouble with the law." I wondered if he had any brushes with the law, before or after the Houdini incident. I had not yet succeeded in positively linking him with any spiritualist group. The idea that he was hired to attack Houdini was still only theory.

At the National Archives in Ottawa I had made some checks with federal penitentiary records, but found nothing on Whitehead. I had written to the RCMP divisions in Montreal and Kelowna, but his name didn't show up in their records. Montreal city police files didn't go back that far.

I found Whitehead in the City of Montreal judicial archives office on Bleury Street, after a couple of hours intense combing through thick annual ledgers which contained the names, listed alphabetically, of everyone who appeared before a criminal court in Montreal since the turn of the twentieth century.

Gordon Whitehead. 1928. Case Number 9949. Found guilty of stealing a book on December 22, value $7.50, from Henry Morgan Department Store. Sentenced to six days in prison and ordered to return the book. Arrest carried out by the store detective Jean M. Robillard. The title of the volume was not given.

Gordon is also named in a dossier dated December 24, 1928 which tells of a raid carried out at 522 Sherbrooke West in the home of a "W. Whitehead" after police received a tip from an anonymous party "acting in good faith." Police seized four books, all shoplifted from Morgan's. The first two were volumes 1 and 2 of *The Diary of Samuel Pepys*. What could have been his interest in Pepys, the philandering seventeenth-century British diarist? The title of the third book was *Famous Prize Fights.* I found a copy at the McGill Library. Subtitled *Epics of the Fancy,* the 260-age illustrated book was written by Jeffery Farnol and published by Little Brown in Boston in 1928. The fourth book, curiously, was *The Hand and the Mind.* By M.N. Laffan, its subject is palmistry. Only ninety-five pages long and with eight plates, it was published in New York by Dutton in 1928.

These, then, were the books that we know were in Whitehead's life, along with *Ideal Marriage* and *Neurosis and Human Growth,* that were bequeathed to Bert McConnell.

Who was W. Whitehead in whose apartment Gordon was living when police confiscated the shoplifted material?

The address was that of the newly-built Wickham Apartments, located not far from the McGill Union. In 1928, according to *Lovell's,* only five apartments were occupied, none by anyone named Whitehead. The next year it was filling up, but again there were no Whiteheads. Gordon and W. Whitehead must have been short-term tenants, or guests of someone else.

A check through *Old McGill* turned up a Wallace Whitehead from Farnham, in Quebec's Eastern Townships. He studied dentistry in the 1920s. After graduating he opened an office in the Medical Arts building at Sherbrooke and Guy. But there is no trace of him in any of McGill's alumni registers. In the 1946 Directory of Graduates, there is only an asterisk beside his name denoting "Address Unknown"; the Order of Dentists of Quebec had an old address for him in Ottawa, but he was long gone from there.

His graduation photo in *Old McGill* shows a handsome young man with an intense look and dark stiffly-parted hair. He played hockey on McGill's senior team, was president of Scarlet Key and chairman of the Junior Prom Committee. He was a member of the Old Scouts Club. Beside his picture was the slogan: "Once a Scout, always a Scout."

45

Something to Remember Him By

In November 1996 I discovered that it is reasonably certain that White-head was seen in Sutton, Quebec. His long coat was something he was remembered by. I was at the Jennings home in the maple forest outside Glen Sutton, the outlaw village where Frank James of the Jesse James gang once holed up, ten miles over the winding mountain road from Sutton. I'd been invited by a book collector friend, John Jennings, to look over the works owned by his father Jack, a retired customs inspector who had passed away. John was intrigued by all the coincidences in my Houdini research.

"It's like fate with a grand purpose, isn't it?" he reflected.

Just then his mother, Norma Jennings, walked in.

"Didn't you know the Jaquays?" John asked his mother.

"The Jaquays? Sure."

"Did you know Mabel Jackson?"

"Of course. Mabel Jackson. That goes a long way back. The early 1950s. She stayed with the Jaquays and was part of a threesome with Mort Jaquays's first wife, Constance, and his second wife, Dorothy. The three were inseparable, always together."

Norma had a photographic memory. She was sure it was around 1952 or 1953 that she saw them—in other words, before Whitehead died in 1954. She and her husband and three sons had moved to Sutton in 1952. She started to notice the three ladies on the street "because they were so different from the rest of us. There was a gentleman with a long coat who was sometimes part of their group. Constance was quite tall, Dorothy was chunky, and I have this vision of Mabel Jackson having sleepy hooded eyes and pudgy cheeks with high colour, not that she wore makeup.

"They were a weird group. All of them wore flat shoes and short dresses with these long colourful golf stockings up to their knees which was considered very avant garde. They were looked upon by the people in the village as the hoity-toity rich of Montreal.

"Dorothy and Mabel wore ponchos—those big heavy capes thrown over their shoulders. They were way ahead of their time compared to everyone else in the village, and they acted weird as well, like they were a cut above the rest of us, like we were just the poor country yokels. Most people in Sutton were prudish and mistrusted outsiders and didn't associate with them."

Did Dorothy communicate with spirits or hold séances?

"That I wouldn't know. Most of our conversations were about health foods and her involvement in the Montessori education system. At that time it wasn't my belief and maybe she realized that, so we just didn't talk about it. But I recall that Mort Jacquays, after he and his first wife split up, had brought over a master baker from England, Bernard Norwood, to please Dorothy because this baker could do health bread. He started the Paramount Farms Bakery on the Jaquays' land. He was also a mystic. One time I told him that I was psychic. He said, 'You can enlarge upon it, you know, you can study it. You can communicate with the dead and see and hear things.' He wanted me to go with him to Montreal, something to do with séances and speaking to the dead."

I returned a few days later with the photograph of Whitehead. Norma studied the picture.

"The hat, the way he wears it, looks very familiar. I'm quite sure it's the same person I used to see walking with the three women. My vision of him is someone tall and slim with a fedora hat which he wore at an angle, slanted down over his right eye, and a long scruffy raincoat. Does that make sense?

"I have the impression," she continued, "that his hair was long and grey, sort of scraggly. He was gaunt, not clean-looking. I have an overall picture of shabbiness. At the time I thought, what in heaven's name is he doing with these three women who were all dressed so hoity-toity with their expensive clothes? And I think he must have lost a lot of weight because he seemed belted in quite tight."

If it was Whitehead she had seen on the street, he was possibly already ill.

"My memory is of him walking with them on Main Street in front of the Mountain View Hotel and the general store and the bank. He was always walking on the inside, hugging the buildings. Dorothy was always in the middle. I'm not making this up. It's exactly what I see in my mind. I remember them going into Ouimet's food store which was next to what is now the gas station."

Ouimet's, which later became the Provigo supermarket, was located across the street from where I was living when I started this project.

Amazingly, as they say, the trail was ending where it started, at home.

46

Eddie Do-Nothing

~

AT ONE POINT while I was engaged in sleuthing around Sutton, Quebec, the CBC-TV *City Beat* crew came to do a story on my obsession. Cameras tagging along, I went into my local post office. When you're on the Houdini case, you never know what surprises may be found in the post office box and what your spontaneous reaction will be. This was a letter, in a small white envelope with no return address. "Hmm," I said into the pea-sized microphone clipped to my shirt pocket, "I wonder who this is from." I opened the letter. It was from Eddie Baker, the subject of a 1970s essay of mine called "The Story of Eddie Do-Nothing" on his mastery of vacuity and inertia. He had made a noble art out of lassitude, but had taken the pains to write. I read the letter out loud to the CBC crew.

I have some very occult authentic unprecedented information concerning Houdini. I feel you are the only person worthy of receiving this precious revelation. It is this:

Houdini is engaged in an erotic liaison with Elvis Presley and Menachim Begin in a pink stucco villa on the scenic shore of the Dead Sea not far from where John the Baptist baptized Jesus Christ in the River Jordan 7 ½ kilometres south of Jericho in the State of Israel.

HONEST.

Well, it's as good a take as any on Houdini.

Harry Houdini and wife Bess.
Courtesy of "Magic Tom" Auburn Collection

Don Bell
1936-2003

Index